P9-DXH-920

The Way of the Shaman

Related Titles from Harper & Row

Wallace Black Elk and William S. Lyon
Black Elk: The Sacred Ways of a Lakota

Percy Bullchild
The Sun Came Down

Carl A. Hammerschlag, M.D.
The Dancing Healers: A Doctor's Journey of Healing with Native Americans

Jamake Highwater
Ritual of the Wind: North American Indian Ceremonies, Music and Dance

Ptolemy Tompkins
*This Tree Grows Out of Hell: Mesoamerica and the Search for the
    Magical Body*

Alberto Villoldo and Erik Jendresen
The Four Winds: A Shaman's Odyssey into the Amazon

The Way of
the Shaman

Michael Harner

HarperSanFrancisco
A Division of HarperCollins*Publishers*

The shamanic way of healing presented in this book should not be considered an exclusive method of confronting medical problems. It should be viewed as an adjunct to orthodox medical or psychological treatment, unless contrary medical advice is given.

THE WAY OF THE SHAMAN: Tenth Anniversary Edition.
Copyright © 1980, 1990 by Michael Harner. Printed in the United States of America. No part of this book may be used or reproduced in any manner whatsoever without written permission except in the case of brief quotations embodied in critical articles and reviews. For information address HarperCollins Publishers, 10 East 53rd Street, New York, NY 10022.

THIRD EDITION
ORIGINALLY PUBLISHED BY HARPER & ROW IN 1980.
FIRST HARPER & ROW PAPERBACK EDITION PUBLISHED IN 1990.

Library of Congress Cataloging-in-Publication Data

Harner, Michael J.
    The way of the shaman / Michael Harner.—10th anniversary ed.,
3rd ed., 1st Harper & Row paperback ed.
        p.   cm.
    Includes bibliographical references and index.
    ISBN 0–06–250373–1 (pbk. : alk. paper) :
    1. Mental healing.   2. Shamanism.   I. Title.
RZ401.H187   1990
615.8'52—dc20   89–46444
                                                                      CIP

01 02 RRD-H 30 29

Contents

To Sandra, Terry, and Jim

Acknowledgments

Grateful acknowledgment is made for use of copyrighted material from the following sources: *Spirit, Spirit: Shaman Songs* by David Cloutier. Copyright © 1973 by David Cloutier. Reprinted by permission of the author and Copper Beech Press. "The Hand Game of the Flathead Indians," by Alan P. Merriam. *Journal of American Folklore* 68, 1955. Copyright © 1955 by the American Folklore Society. Reprinted by permission of the author and the American Folklore Society.

I also would like to acknowledge the research assistance of Bruce Woych and Karen Ciatyk, and the advice of my editor, John Loudon, as well as that of my wife, Sandra Harner.

". . . Aboriginal medicine-men, so far from being rogues, charlatans or ignoramuses, are men of *high* degree; that is, men who have taken a degree in the secret life beyond that taken by most adult males—a step which implies discipline, mental training, courage and perseverance . . . they are men of respected, and often of outstanding, personality . . . they are of immense social significance, the psychological health of the group largely depending on faith in their powers . . . the various psychic powers attributed to them must not be too readily dismissed as mere primitive magic and 'makebelieve,' for many of them have specialized in the working of the human mind, and in the influence of mind on body and of mind on mind . . ."

From *Aboriginal Men of High Degree* by the late Australian anthropologist A. P. Elkin (1945:78-79)

Preface to the Third Edition

Ten years have passed since the original edition of this book appeared,[1] and they have been remarkable years indeed for the shamanic renaissance. Before then, shamanism was rapidly disappearing from the Planet as missionaries, colonists, governments, and commercial interests overwhelmed tribal peoples and their ancient cultures. During the last decade, however, shamanism has returned to human life with startling strength, even to urban strongholds of Western "civilization," such as New York and Vienna. This resurgence has come so subtly that most of the public is probably unaware that there is such a thing as shamanism, let alone conscious of its return. There is another public, however, rapidly-growing and now numbering in the thousands in the United States and abroad, that has taken up shamanism and made it a part of personal daily life.[2]

The return of shamanism has perplexed many observers outside of the movement, so I would like to suggest a few of the factors contributing to this revival. One reason for the increasing interest in shamanism is that many educated, thinking people have left the Age of Faith behind them. They no longer trust ecclesiastical dogma and authority to provide them with adequate evidence of the realms of the spirit or, indeed, with evidence that there is spirit. Secondhand or thirdhand anecdotes in competing and culture-bound religious texts from other times and places are not convincing enough to provide paradigms for their personal existence. They require higher standards of evidence.

The "New Age" is partially an offshoot of the Age of Science, bringing into personal life the paradigmatic consequences of two centuries of serious use of the scientific method. These children of the Age of Science, myself included, prefer to arrive first-hand, experimentally, at their own conclusions as to the nature and limits of reality. Shamanism provides a way to conduct these personal experiments, for it is a methodology, not a religion.

The Age of Science produced LSD, and many who have come to shamanism had already conducted "experiments," albeit informally, with psychedelic drug "trips," but found they had no framework or discipline within which to place their experiences. They searched in the books of Castaneda and others for road maps of their experiences, and sensed the secret cartography lay in shamanism.

The Age of Science also produced the NDE (near-death experience) on a large scale, due to a new level of medical technology that has permitted millions of Americans to be revived from a clinically-defined state of death. Near-death experiences, although unplanned, have turned out also to be personal experiments that tested, and commonly changed, the NDE survivors' previous assumptions about reality and the existence of spirit. These people, too, searched for maps, and many have turned to the ancient shamanic methods in the course of their search.

Shamanic methods require a relaxed discipline, with concentration and purpose. Contemporary shamanism, like that in most tribal cultures, typically utilizes monotonous percussion sound to enter an altered state of consciousness. This classic drug-free method is remarkably safe. If practitioners do not maintain focus and discipline, they simply return to the ordinary state of consciousness. There is no preordained period of altered state of consciousness that would tend to occur with a psychedelic drug.

At the same time, the classic shamanic methods work surprisingly quickly, with the result that most persons can achieve in a few hours experiences that might otherwise take them years of silent meditation, prayer, or chanting. For this reason alone, shamanism is ideally suited to the contemporary life of busy people, just as it was suited, for example, to the Eskimo (Inuit) people whose daily hours were filled with tasks of struggle for survival, but whose evenings could be used for shamanism.

Another factor in the return of shamanism is the recent development of holistic health approaches actively utilizing the mind to help healing and the maintenance of wellness. Many of the New Age practices in the holistic health field represent the rediscovery, through recent experimentation, of methods once widely known in tribal and folk practice. Shamanism, as a system embodying much of this ancient knowledge, is gaining increasing attention from those seeking new solutions to health problems, whether defined as physical or mental-emotional.[3] Specific techniques long used in shamanism, such as change in state of consciousness, stress-reduction, visualization, positive thinking, and assistance from nonordinary sources, are some of the approaches now widely employed in contemporary holistic practice.

Another important reason that shamanism has wide appeal today is that it is spiritual ecology. In this time of worldwide environmental crisis, shamanism provides something largely lacking in the anthropocentric ''great'' religions: reverence for, and spiritual communication with, the other beings of the Earth and with the Planet itself. In shamanism, this is not simple Nature worship, but a two-way spiritual communication that resurrects the lost connections our human ancestors had with the awesome spiritual power and beauty of our garden Earth. The shamans, as the late distinguished scholar of shamanism and comparative religion Mircea Eliade points out, are the last humans able to talk with the animals.[4] Indeed, I would add that they are the last ones able to talk with all of Nature, including the plants, the streams, the air, and the rocks. Our ancient hunting and gathering ancestors recognized that their environment held the power of life and death over them, and considered such communication essential for their survival.

Now we, too, are starting to recognize the power of life and death that our environment holds over us. After incredibly reckless and merciless destruction of the other species of the Planet, of the quality of air, water, and the earth itself, we are returning to an awareness, however slowly, that the ultimate survival of our species depends on respecting our Planetary environment. But respect alone is not enough. We need to communicate intimately and lovingly with ''all our relations,'' as the Lakota would say, talking not just with the human people, but also with the animal people, the plant people, and all the elements of the environment, including the soil, the rocks, and the water. In fact, from the shaman's viewpoint, our surroundings are not ''environment,'' but family.

Today, from Zurich to Auckland, from Chicago to São Paulo, humans are again taking up the ancient way of the shaman, often in drumming circles or groups which meet regularly for practice and healing work.

These groups are autonomous—working, as shamans have from time immemorial, independently in small communities to learn, help themselves, and help others. And these informal communities are part of a larger community now truly international but without hierarchy or dogma, for the spiritual authorities, as in tribal times, are found directly in nonordinary reality by each individual shamanic journeyer.

The drumming circles typically meet weekly or biweekly in the evening and usually number between three and twelve people, with leadership and drumming responsibilities rotated. By working together, the participants not only provide live drumming, but engage in shamanic work to help each other as well as friends and relatives. If the group does healing work for others, it does the work without charge as a spiritual service.

Many other persons primarily work alone, outside of drumming groups, using a stereo cassette player, headphones, and drumming tape designed for shamanic journeying. When employed correctly, the drumming tape can be surprisingly effective (see Appendix A). The tape, along with other technological and methodological features, is also used in a problem-solving system called "shamanic counseling."[5]

Using the core or fundamental methods of shamanism emphasized in this book and in my shamanic training workshops, these new practitioners are not "playing Indian," but going to the same revelatory spiritual sources that tribal shamans have traveled to from time immemorial. They are not pretending to be shamans; if they get shamanic results for themselves and others in this work, they are indeed the real thing. Their experiences are genuine and, when described, are essentially interchangeable with the accounts of shamans from nonliterate tribal cultures. The shamanic work is the same, the human mind, heart, and body are the same; only the cultures are different.

Pursuing their shamanic practices, they have come to realize that what most people describe as "reality" only barely touches the grandeur, power, and mystery of the universe. The new shamans often cry tears of ecstasy when undergoing and recounting their experiences. They talk with mutual understanding to persons who have had near-death experiences, and see hope where others may see hopelessness.

They tend to undergo transformation as they discover the incredible safety and love of the normally-hidden universe. The cosmic love they repeatedly encounter in their journeys is increasingly expressed in their daily lives. They are not lonely, even if alone, for they have come to understand that we are never really isolated. Like Siberian shamans, they realize, "Everything that is, is alive!" Everywhere they are surrounded by life, by family. They have returned to the eternal community of the shaman, unlimited by the boundaries of space and time.

Michael Harner
Norwalk, Connecticut
Spring 1990

Introduction

Shamans—whom we in the "civilized" world have called "medicine
men" and "witch doctors"—are the keepers of a remarkable body of
ancient techniques that they use to achieve and maintain well-being and
healing for themselves and members of their communities. These
shamanic methods are strikingly similar the world over, even for peoples
whose cultures are quite different in other respects, and who have been
separated by oceans and continents for tens of thousands of years.

These so-called primitive peoples lacked our advanced level of
medical technology, so they had excellent reason to be motivated to
develop the nontechnological capacities of the human mind for health
and healing. The basic uniformity of shamanic methods suggests that,
through trial and error, people arrived at the same conclusions.

Shamanism is a great mental and emotional adventure, one in which
the patient as well as the shaman-healer are involved. Through his
heroic journey and efforts, the shaman helps his patients transcend their
normal, ordinary definition of reality, including the definition of
themselves as ill. The shaman shows his patients that they are not
emotionally and spiritually alone in their struggles against illness and
death. The shaman shares his special powers and convinces his patients,
on a deep level of consciousness, that another human is willing
to offer up his own self to help them. The shaman's self-sacrifice calls
forth a commensurate emotional commitment from his patients, a sense

of obligation to struggle alongside the shaman to save one's self. Caring and curing go hand in hand.

Today we are discovering that even the near-miracles of modern Western medicine are not always adequate in themselves to solve completely all the problems of those who are ill or who wish to avoid illness. Increasingly, health professionals and their patients are seeking supplementary healing methods, and many healthy individuals are also engaged in personal experimentation to discover workable alternative approaches to achieving well-being. In this experimentation it is often difficult for the layman or even the health professional to distinguish the spurious from the effective. In contrast, the ancient methods of shamanism are already time-tested; in fact, they have been tested immeasurably longer, for example, than psychoanalysis and a variety of other psychotherapeutic techniques. One purpose of this book is to help contemporary Westerners, for the first time, to benefit from this knowledge in their quest to supplement the approaches of modern technological medicine.

By employing the methods described in this book, you will have an opportunity to acquire the experience of shamanic power and to help yourself and others. In my training workshops in shamanic power and healing in North America and Europe, students have demonstrated again and again that most Westerners can easily become initiated into the fundamentals of shamanic practice. The ancient way is so powerful, and taps so deeply into the human mind, that one's usual cultural belief systems and assumptions about reality are essentially irrelevant.

Some may question whether shamanism can be learned from a book. To a certain degree the question is justified; ultimately, shamanic knowledge can only be acquired through individual experience. You must learn the methods in order to utilize them, however. They can be learned in a variety of ways. For example, among the Conibo of the Upper Amazon, "learning from the trees" is considered superior to learning from another shaman. In aboriginal Siberia, a death/rebirth experience was often a major source of shamanic knowledge. In certain preliterate cultures, persons spontaneously answer the "call" of shamanism without any formal training, while in others they train under the guidance of a practicing shaman anywhere from a day to five years or more.

In Western culture, most people will never know a shaman, let alone train with one. Yet, since ours is a literate culture, you do not have to be in an apprenticeship situation to learn; a written guide can provide the essential methodological information. Although it may seem awkward at first to learn basic shamanic techniques from a book, persist. Your shamanic experiences will prove their own value. As in any other field of learning, of course, it is enhancing to work firsthand with a professional. Those who wish such an experience may participate in training workshops (see Appendix A).

In shamanism, the maintenance of one's personal power is fundamental to well-being. The book will introduce you to some of the basic shamanic methods of restoring and maintaining personal power, and using it to help others who are weak, ill, or injured. The techniques are simple and powerful. Their use does not require "faith" nor changes in the assumptions you have about reality in your ordinary state of consciousness. Indeed, the system usually does not even require change in your unconscious mind either, for it only awakens what is already there. However, while the basic techniques of shamanism are simple and relatively easy to learn, the effective practice of shamanism requires self-discipline and dedication.

In engaging in shamanic practice, one moves between what I term an Ordinary State of Consciousness (OSC) and a Shamanic State of Consciousness (SSC). These states of consciousness are the keys to understanding, for example, how Carlos Castaneda can speak of an "ordinary reality" and a "nonordinary reality." The difference in these states of consciousness can perhaps be illustrated by referring to animals. Dragons, griffins, and other animals that would be considered "mythical" by us in the OSC are "real" in the SSC. The idea that there are "mythical" animals is a useful and valid construct in OSC life, but superfluous and irrelevant in SSC experiences. "Fantasy" can be said to be a term applied by a person in the OSC to what is experienced in the SSC. Conversely, a person in the SSC may perceive the experiences of the OSC to be illusory in SSC terms. Both are right, as viewed from their own particular states of consciousness.

The shaman has the advantage of being able to move between states of consciousness at will. He can enter the OSC of the nonshaman and honestly agree with him about the nature of reality from that perspective. Then the shaman can return to the SSC and obtain firsthand confirmation of the testimony of others who have reported on their experiences in that state.

Observation with one's own senses is the basis for the empirical definition of reality; and there is no one yet, even in the sciences of ordinary reality, who has uncontestably proven that there is only one state of consciousness that is valid for firsthand observations. The myth of the SSC is ordinary reality; and the myth of the OSC is nonordinary reality. It is extremely difficult for an unprejudiced judgement to be made about the validity of the experiences in the contrasting state of consciousness.

To understand the deep-seated, emotional hostility that greeted the works of Castaneda in some quarters, one needs to keep in mind that this kind of prejudice is often involved. It is the counterpart of ethnocentrism between cultures. But in this case it is not the narrowness of someone's *cultural* experience that is the fundamental issue, but the narrowness of someone's *conscious* experience. The persons most prejudiced against a concept of nonordinary reality are those who have never experienced it. This might be termed *cognicentrism,* the analogue in consciousness of ethnocentrism.

A step in the direction toward a solution of this problem may well be for more persons to become shamans, so that they may experience the SSC for themselves, and on their own terms. Such shamans, as they have done from time immemorial in other cultures, can then communicate an understanding of that nonordinary reality to those who have never entered it. This would be comparable to the role of the anthropologist who, by undertaking participant observation in a culture other than his own, is subsequently able to communicate an understanding of that culture to people who would otherwise view it as alien, incomprehensible, and inferior.

Anthropologists teach others to try to avoid the pitfalls of ethnocentrism by learning to understand a culture in terms of its own assumptions about reality. Western shamans can do a similar service with regard to cognicentrism. The anthropologists' lesson is called *cultural relativism.* What Western shamans can try to create, to some degree, is *cognitive relativism.* Later, when an empirical knowledge of the experiences of the SSC is achieved, there may be a respect for its own assumptions. Then the time will perhaps be ripe for unprejudiced analysis of SSC experiences scientifically in OSC terms.

Some might argue that the reason we humans spend most of our waking lives in the OSC is that natural selection intended it that way because that is the *real* reality, and that other states of consciousness, other than sleep, are aberrations that interfere with our survival. In other words, such an argument might go, we perceive reality the way we usually do because that is always the best way in terms of survival. But recent advances in neurochemistry show that the human brain carries its own consciousness-altering drugs, including hallucinogens such as dimethyltryptamine.[1] In terms of natural selection, it seems unlikely that they would be present unless their capacity to alter the state of consciousness could confer some advantage for survival. It would appear that Nature itself has made a decision that an altered state of consciousness is sometimes superior to an ordinary state.

We are only beginning in the West to start appreciating the important impact the state of the mind can have on what have previously been too often perceived as questions of purely "physical" capability. When, in an emergency, an Australian aborigine shaman or a Tibetan lama engages in "fast traveling"—a trance or SSC technique for running long distances at a rapid rate—that is clearly a survival technique which, by definition, is not possible in the OSC.[2]

Similarly, we now are learning that many of our finest athletes enter an altered state of consciousness when they are making their greatest achievements. All in all, it seems inappropriate to argue that only a single state of consciousness is superior under all circumstances. The shaman has long known that such an assumption is not only false, but dangerous to health and well-being. The shaman, using millenia of accumulated knowledge as well as his firsthand experiences, knows when a change in state of consciousness is appropriate and even necessary.

In the SSC the shaman not only experiences what is impossible in the OSC, but does it. Even if it should be proven that all the shaman experiences in the SSC is purely in his mind, that would not make that realm any less real to him. Indeed, such a conclusion would mean that the shaman's experiences and deeds are *not* impossible in any absolute sense.

The exercises presented in this book represent my own personal distillation and interpretation of some of the millennia-old shamanic methods that I have learned firsthand from South and North American Indians, supplemented by information from the ethnographic literature, including that from other continents. I have adapted the methods so that Western readers, regardless of their religious or philosophical orientations, may use the techniques in daily life. The methods are for those in good health as well as those "dis-spirited" or otherwise ill. From the viewpoint of shamanism, personal power is basic to health under all conditions of one's life.

To benefit seriously from the book, you should be careful to undertake the exercises or experiences precisely in the sequence presented, not attempting a subsequent exercise until success has been achieved with the preceding one. Sometimes it is possible for a person to attain all these stages in a few days; more commonly it takes weeks or months. The important thing is not speed but constant personal practice. As long as you proceed in a disciplined way to practice the methods you have learned, you are in the process of becoming a shaman. And at what point *are* you a shaman? That status can only be conferred on you by those you attempt to help in matters of power and healing. In other words, it is recognized success in shamanic work that determines whether you have indeed become a shaman.

You will have the opportunity to find that, completely without the use of drugs, you can alter your state of consciousness in classic shamanic ways and enter the nonordinary reality of shamanism. There in the SSC, you may become a seer (*see-er*), and undertake personally the famed shamanic journey to acquire firsthand knowledge of a hidden universe. You can also discover how to benefit from your journeys in terms of healing and health, using ancient methods that both foreshadow and go beyond Western psychology, medicine, and spirituality. In addition, you can learn nonjourneying methods through which one maintains and improves personal power.

It is not unusual for Westerners to approach shamanic exercises for the first time with some trepidation. Yet in every case I know, anxieties have soon been replaced by feelings of discovery, positive excitement, and self-confidence. It is no accident that the term *ecstasy* commonly refers both to the shamanic "trance" or SSC and to a state of exaltation or rapturous delight. The shamanic experience is a positive one, as has been verified through thousands of years, and as I have seen again and again in my training workshops, in which the participants have represented a wide spectrum of personalities.

The SSC, it can be said, is safer than dreaming. In a dream, you may not be able to extricate yourself voluntarily from an unwanted experience or nightmare. In contrast, one wills himself into the SSC and, since it is a conscious waking state, is able at any time to will himself out of it, back into the OSC. Unlike a psychedelic drug experience, there is no chemically determined length of time that one must be in an altered state of consciousness, and no possibility of being locked into a "bad trip." The only significant dangers I know of connected with the practice of shamanism are social or political. For example, it was obviously dangerous to be a shaman in Europe during the time of the Inquisition, and even today among the Jívaro it can be dangerous to be accused of being a "bad" or bewitching shaman, a practitioner of a type of shamanism not taught here.

This is essentially a phenomenological presentation. I will not be trying to explain away shamanic concepts and practices in the terms of psychoanalysis or any other contemporary Western system of causal theory. The causality involved in shamanism and shamanic healing is, indeed, a very interesting question, and a question worthy of intensive research, but causality-oriented scientific research is not essential to teaching shamanic practice—the main objective here. In other words, Western questions as to why shamanism works are not necessary in order to experience and employ the methods.

Try to suspend any critical prejudgments as you first practice shamanic methods. Simply enjoy the adventures of the shamanic approach; absorb and practice what you read, and then see where your explorations take you. For days, weeks, and perhaps years after you have used these methods, you will have ample time for reflecting on their meaning from a Western point of view. The effective way to learn the shamans' system is to use the same basic concepts they do. For example, when I speak of "spirits," it is because that is the way shamans talk within the system. To practice shamanism, it is unnecessary and even distracting to be preoccupied with achieving a scientific understanding of what "spirits" may really represent and why shamanism works.

The books of Carlos Castaneda, regardless of the questions that have been raised regarding their degree of fictionalization, have performed the valuable service of introducing many Westerners to the adventure and excitement of shamanism and to some of the legitimate principles involved. In the pages that follow I will not recapitulate the materials in Castaneda's works, nor have I set myself the task of showing equivalences between his concepts and the ones presented here. For most readers of his books, however, many of the parallels should be fairly obvious. One of the things I should note, however, is that Castaneda does not emphasize healing in his books, although this is generally one of the most important tasks of shamanism. Perhaps this is because his don Juan is basically engaged in the warrior (or sorcerer) type of shamanism.

The main focus here is to provide an introductory handbook of shamanic methodology for health and healing. There is much more that I could write, and perhaps I will in the future, but the basic essentials are here for anyone who has the capacity and inclination to start becoming a shaman. A knowledge of shamanism, like any knowledge, can be used for different ends, depending upon the way it is employed. The way I offer you is that of the healer, not of the sorcerer, and the methods given are those for achieving well-being and health, and for helping others.

Finally, I should state, if it is not already obvious, that I practice shamanism myself; not because I understand in OSC terms *why* it works, but simply because it *does* work. But don't take my word for it: truly significant shamanic knowledge is *experienced,* and cannot be obtained from me or any other shaman. Shamanism is, after all, basically a strategy for personal learning and acting on that learning. I offer you a portion of that strategy and welcome you to the ancient shamanic adventure.

The Way of the Shaman

CHAPTER 1

Discovering the Way

My first prolonged fieldwork as an anthropologist took place in 1956 and 1957 on the forested eastern slopes of the Ecuadorian Andes among the Jívaro [HEE-varo] Indians, or *Untsuri Shuar*. The Jívaro were famous at that time for their now essentially vanished practice of "head-shrinking," and for their intensive practice of shamanism, which still continues. I successfully collected a great deal of information, but remained an outside observer of the world of the shaman at that time.

A couple of years later, the American Museum of Natural History invited me to make a year-long expedition to the Peruvian Amazon to study the culture of the Conibo Indians of the Ucayali River region. I accepted, delighted to have an opportunity to do more research on the fascinating Upper Amazon forest cultures. That fieldwork took place in 1960 and 1961.

Two particular experiences I had among the Conibo and the Jívaro were basic to my discovering the way of the shaman in both those cultures, and I would like to share them with you. Perhaps they will convey something of the incredible hidden world open to the shamanic explorer.

I had been living for the better part of a year in a Conibo Indian village beside a remote lake off a tributary of the Río Ucayali. My anthropological research on the culture of the Conibo had been going well, but my attempts to elicit information on their religion met with little success. The people were friendly, but reluctant to talk about the supernatural. Finally they told me that if I really wished to learn, I must take the shamans' sacred drink made from *ayahuasca,* the "soul vine." I agreed, with both curiosity and trepidation, for they warned me that the experience would be very frightening.

The next morning my friend Tomás, the kind elder of the village, went into the forest to cut the vines. Before leaving, he told me to fast: a light breakfast and no lunch. He returned midday with enough *ayahuasca* vines and leaves of the *cawa* plant to fill a fifteen gallon pot. He boiled them all afternoon, until only about a quart of dark liquid remained. This he poured into an old bottle and left it to cool until sunset, when he said we would drink it.

The Indians muzzled the dogs in the village so that they could not bark. The noise of barking dogs could drive a man who had taken *ayahuasca* mad, I was told. The children were cautioned to be quiet, and silence came over the small community with the setting of the sun.

As the brief equatorial twilight was replaced by darkness, Tomás poured about a third of the bottle into a gourd bowl and gave it to me. All the Indians were watching. I felt like Socrates amidst his Athenian compatriots, accepting the hemlock—it occurred to me that one of the alternate names people in the Peruvian Amazon gave *ayahuasca* was "the little death." I drank the potion quickly. It had a strange, slightly bitter taste. I then waited for Tomás to take his turn, but he said that he had decided not to participate after all.

They had me lie down on the bamboo platform under the great thatched roof of the communal house. The village was silent, except for the chirping of crickets and the distant calls of a howler monkey deep in the jungle.

As I stared upward into the darkness, faint lines of light appeared. They grew sharper, more intricate, and burst into brilliant colors. Sound came from far away, a sound like a waterfall, which grew stronger and stronger until it filled my ears.

Just a few minutes earlier I had been disappointed, sure that the *ayahuasca* was not going to have any effect on me. Now the sound of rushing water flooded my brain. My jaw began to feel numb, and the numbness was moving up to my temples.

2

Overhead the faint lines became brighter, and gradually interlaced to form a canopy resembling a geometric mosaic of stained glass. The bright violet hues formed an ever-expanding roof above me. Within this celestial cavern, I heard the sound of water grow louder and I could see dim figures engaged in shadowy movements. As my eyes seemed to adjust to the gloom, the moving scene resolved itself into something resembling a huge fun house, a supernatural carnival of demons. In the center, presiding over the activities, and looking directly at me, was a gigantic, grinning crocodilian head, from whose cavernous jaws gushed a torrential flood of water. Slowly the waters rose, and so did the canopy above them, until the scene metamorphosed into a simple duality of blue sky above and sea below. All creatures had vanished.

Then, from my position near the surface of the water, I began to see two strange boats wafting back and forth, floating through the air towards me, coming closer and closer. They slowly combined to form a single vessel with a huge dragon-headed prow, not unlike that of a Viking ship. Set amidships was a square sail. Gradually, as the boat gently floated back and forth above me, I heard a rhythmic swishing sound and saw that it was a giant galley with several hundred oars moving back and forth in cadence with the sound.

I became conscious, too, of the most beautiful singing I have ever heard in my life, high-pitched and ethereal, emanating from myriad voices on board the galley. As I looked more closely at the deck, I could make out large numbers of people with the heads of blue jays and the bodies of humans, not unlike the bird-headed gods of ancient Egyptian tomb paintings. At the same time, some energy-essence began to float from my chest up into the boat. Although I believed myself to be an atheist, I was completely certain that I was dying and that the bird-headed people had come to take my soul away on the boat. While the soul-flow continued from my chest, I was aware that the extremities of my body were growing numb.

Starting with my arms and legs, my body slowly began to feel like it was turning to solid concrete. I could not move or speak. Gradually, as the numbness closed in on my chest, toward my heart, I tried to get my mouth to ask for help, to ask the Indians for an antidote. Try as I might, however, I could not marshal my abilities sufficiently to make a word. Simultaneously, my abdomen seemed to be turning to stone, and I had to make a tremendous effort to keep my heart beating. I began to call my heart my friend, my dearest friend of all, to talk to it, to encourage it to beat with all the power remaining at my command.

I became aware of my brain. I felt—physically—that it had become compartmentalized into four separate and distinct levels. At the uppermost surface was the observer and commander, which was conscious of the condition of my body, and was responsible for the attempt to keep my heart going. It perceived, but purely as a spectator, the visions emanating from what seemed to be the nether portions of my brain. Immediately below the topmost level I felt a numbed layer, which seemed to have been put out of commission by the drug—it just wasn't there. The next level down was the source of my visions, including the soul boat.

Now I was virtually certain I was about to die. As I tried to accept my fate, an even lower portion of my brain began to transmit more visions and information. I was "told" that this new material was being presented to me because I was dying and therefore "safe" to receive these revelations. These were the secrets reserved for the dying and the dead, I was informed. I could only very dimly perceive the givers of these thoughts: giant reptilian creatures reposing sluggishly at the lowermost depths of the back of my brain, where it met the top of the spinal column. I could only vaguely see them in what seemed to be gloomy, dark depths.

Then they projected a visual scene in front of me. First they showed me the planet Earth as it was eons ago, before there was any life on it. I saw an ocean, barren land, and a bright blue sky. Then black specks dropped from the sky by the hundreds and landed in front of me on the barren landscape. I could see that the "specks" were actually large, shiny, black creatures with stubby pterodactyl-like wings and huge whale-like bodies. Their heads were not visible to me. They flopped down, utterly exhausted from their trip, resting for eons. They explained to me in a kind of thought language that they were fleeing from something out in space. They had come to the planet Earth to escape their enemy.

The creatures then showed me how they had created life on the planet in order to hide within the multitudinous forms and thus disguise their presence. Before me, the magnificence of plant and animal creation and speciation—hundreds of millions of years of activity—took place on a scale and with a vividness impossible to describe. I learned that the dragon-like creatures were thus inside of all forms of life, including man.* They were the true masters of humanity and the entire

* In retrospect one could say they were almost like DNA, although at that time, 1961, I knew nothing of DNA.

4

planet, they told me. We humans were but the receptacles and servants of these creatures. For this reason they could speak to me from within myself.

These revelations, welling up from the depths of my mind, alternated with visions of the floating galley, which had almost finished taking my soul on board. The boat with its blue-jay headed deck crew was gradually drawing away, pulling my life force along as it headed toward a large fjord flanked by barren, worn hills. I knew I had only a moment more to live. Strangely, I had no fear of the bird-headed people; they were welcome to have my soul if they could keep it. But I was afraid that somehow my soul might not remain on the horizontal plane of the fjord but might, through processes unknown but felt and dreaded, be acquired or re-acquired by the dragon-like denizens of the depths.

I suddenly felt my distinctive humanness, the contrast between my species and the ancient reptilian ancestors. I began to struggle against returning to the ancient ones, who were beginning to feel increasingly alien and possibly evil. Each heart beat was a major undertaking. I turned to human help.

With an unimaginable last effort, I barely managed to utter one word to the Indians: "Medicine!" I saw them rushing around to make an antidote, and I knew they could not prepare it in time. I needed a guardian who could defeat dragons, and I frantically tried to conjure up a powerful being to protect me against the alien reptilian creatures. One appeared before me; and at that moment the Indians forced my mouth open and poured the antidote into me. Gradually, the dragons disappeared back into the lower depths; the soul boat and the fjord were no more. I relaxed with relief.

The antidote radically eased my condition, but it did not prevent me from having many additional visions of a more superficial nature. These were manageable and enjoyable. I made fabulous journeys at will through distant regions, even out into the Galaxy; created incredible architecture; and employed sardonically grinning demons to realize my fantasies. Often I found myself laughing aloud at the incongruities of my adventures.

Finally, I slept.

Rays of sunlight were piercing the holes in the palm-thatched roof when I awoke. I was still lying on the bamboo platform, and I heard the normal, morning sounds all around me: the Indians conversing, babies

5

crying, and a rooster crowing. I was surprised to discover that I felt refreshed and peaceful. As I lay there looking up at the beautiful woven pattern of the roof, the memories of the previous night drifted across my mind. I momentarily stopped myself from remembering more in order to get my tape recorder from a duffle bag. As I dug into the bag, several of the Indians greeted me, smiling. An old woman, Tomás' wife, gave me a bowl of fish and plantain soup for breakfast. It tasted extraordinarily good. Then I went back to the platform, eager to put my night's experiences on tape before I forgot anything.

The work of recall went easily except for one portion of the trance that I could not remember. It remained blank, as though a tape had been erased. I struggled for hours to remember what had happened in that part of the experience, and I virtually wrestled it back into my consciousness. The recalcitrant material turned out to be the communication from the dragon-like creatures, including the revelation of their role in the evolution of life on this planet and their innate domination of living matter, including man. I was highly excited at rediscovering this material, and could not help but feel that I was not supposed to be able to bring it back from the nether regions of the mind.

I even had a peculiar sense of fear for my safety, because I now possessed a secret that the creatures had indicated was only intended for the dying. I immediately decided to share this knowledge with others so that the "secret" would not reside in me alone, and my life would not be in jeopardy. I put my outboard motor on a dugout canoe and left for an American evangelist mission station nearby. I arrived about noon.

The couple at the mission, Bob and Millie, were a cut above the average evangelists sent from the United States: hospitable, humorous, and compassionate.[1] I told them my story. When I described the reptile with water gushing out of his mouth, they exchanged glances, reached for their Bible, and read to me the following line from Chapter 12 in the Book of Revelation:

And the serpent cast out of his mouth water as a flood . . .

They explained to me that the word "serpent" was synonymous in the Bible with the words "dragon" and "Satan." I went on with my narrative. When I came to the part about the dragon-like creatures fleeing an enemy somewhere beyond the Earth and landing here to hide from their pursuers, Bob and Millie became excited and again read me

6

more from the same passage in the Book of Revelation:

And there was a war in heaven: Michael and his angels fought against the dragon; and the dragon fought and his angels. And prevailed not; neither was their place found any more in heaven. And the great dragon was cast out, that old serpent, called the Devil, and Satan, which deceiveth the whole world: he was cast out into the earth, and his angels with him.

I listened with surprise and wonder. The missionaries, in turn, seemed to be awed by the fact that an atheistic anthropologist, by taking the drink of the "witch doctors," could apparently have revealed to him some of the same holy material in the Book of Revelation. When I had finished my account, I was relieved to have shared my new knowledge, but I was also exhausted. I fell asleep on the missionaries' bed, leaving them to continue their discussion of the experience.

That evening, as I returned to the village in my canoe, my head began to throb in rhythm with the noise of the outboard motor; I thought I was going mad; I had to stick my fingers in my ears to avoid the sensation. I slept well, but the next day I noticed a numbness or pressure in my head.

I was now eager to solicit a professional opinion from the most supernaturally knowledgeable of the Indians, a blind shaman who had made many excursions into the spirit world with the aid of the *ayahuasca* drink. It seemed only proper that a blind man might be able to be my guide to the world of darkness.

I went to his hut, taking my notebook with me, and described my visions to him segment by segment. At first I told him only the highlights; thus, when I came to the dragon-like creatures, I skipped their arrival from space and only said, "There were these giant black animals, something like great bats, longer than the length of this house, who said that they were the true masters of the world." There is no word for dragon in Conibo, so "giant bat" was the closest I could come to describe what I had seen.

He stared up toward me with his sightless eyes, and said with a grin, "Oh, they're always saying that. But they are only the Masters of Outer Darkness."

He waved his hand casually toward the sky. I felt a chill along the lower part of my spine, for I had not yet told him that I had seen them, in my trance, coming from outer space.

I was stunned. What I had experienced was already familiar to this

7

barefoot, blind shaman. Known to him from his own explorations of the same hidden world into which I had ventured. From that moment on I decided to learn everything I could about shamanism.

And there was something more that encouraged me in my new quest. After I recounted my entire experience, he told me that he did not know of anyone who had encountered and learned so much on his first *ayahuasca* journey.

"You can surely be a master shaman," he said.

Thus my serious study of shamanism began. From the Conibo I especially learned about the journey into the Lowerworld and the retrieval of spirits, methods that will be described later in the book. I returned to the United States in 1961, but three years later I came back to South America to be with the Jívaro, with whom I had lived in 1956 and 1957. My mission this time was not just to be an anthropologist, but to learn firsthand how to practice shamanism the Jívaro way. For that reason, I wanted to go to the northwestern part of the Jívaro country where the most powerful shamans were reputed to reside.

I first flew to Quito, Ecuador, in the Andean highlands. I took an old Junkers tri-motor down to a jungle airfield at the eastern base of the Andes on the Pastaza River. There I chartered a single-engine plane to Macas, an ancient white settlement at the foot of the Andes in the midst of the Jívaro country.

Macas was a strange village. It had been founded in 1599 by a handful of Spaniards who had survived the massacre of the legendary Sevilla del Oro by the Jívaro, and for centuries had been perhaps the most isolated community of the Western world. Until the airstrip was built in the 1940s, its most direct connection to the outside world had been a slippery footpath over the Andean escarpment west of the village, involving an arduous eight-day hike to reach the highland city of Riobamba. This isolation had created a white community unlike any other in the world. Even during the early years of the twentieth century the men hunted with blowguns, wore Indian dress, and proudly declared their direct descent from the Conquistadores.

They also had their own marvelous legends and private mysteries. For example, there was the story of how, after the massacre and the retreat from Sevilla del Oro, it took them almost a century to find a new way out over the Andes. The man who had finally succeeded was still remembered in bedtime stories to the children. And there was the spectral horse, complete with clanking chains, which was reportedly such a frequent night visitor to the streets of the village that the inhabitants often huddled inside the palm-thatched huts while the monster roamed about. Its visits ended in 1924, when Catholic missionaries permanently settled in the community. At that time, incidentally, there were still no horses in Macas—the first one, a colt, was carried in on a man's back from Riobamba in 1928, almost three and a half centuries after the community's founding.

Up behind the village, surmounting the eastern Cordillera of the Andes, was Sangay, a great active volcano, snow-capped, billowing smoke by day and glowing by night. The glow, the Macabeos liked to say, was produced by the treasure of the Incas, which they claimed was buried on the slopes of Sangay.

My first day in Macas went well. My young Jívaro guide was awaiting me at the airstrip and the people were hospitable and generous. Food was plentiful, and our meals included generous portions of meat. Since there was no way for the Macabeos to get their cattle over the Andes, they had to eat the beasts themselves; thus cattle were slaughtered in the little village every day. In addition, they gave me *guayusa,* a native tea, which the Macabeos consumed throughout the day instead of coffee. The tea created a sense of euphoria, and the entire local population was gently stoned all day. *Guayusa* is so habituating that before it is offered to a visitor, he is warned that once he drinks it, he will ever after always return to the Ecuadorian jungle.

As I drifted off to sleep in Macas that night of my arrival, images in brilliant reddish hues appeared to me in the darkness of the Macabeo house. What I saw was most peculiar: curvilinear designs intertwining, separating, and turning in a most enjoyable fashion. Then small, grinning demonic faces, which were also red, appeared among the changing patterns—swirling, disappearing and reappearing. I felt I was seeing the spiritual inhabitants of Macas.

Suddenly, with an explosion and a jolt, I was almost thrown off my slat bed. The dogs of the village burst out barking. The visions vanished. People were shouting. An earthquake had shaken the ground, and now a spray of natural fireworks shot into the night sky from Sangay. I felt, undoubtedly irrationally, that the sardonic demons had produced the eruption to greet my return to the jungle and to remind me of their reality. I laughed to myself at the absurdity of it all.

The next day the Catholic missionary showed me his private

9

collection of prehistoric potsherds from the local area. On them were painted red designs almost identical to those I had seen the previous night.

The following morning, my Jívaro guide and I walked northward from Macas, crossed the Río Upano in a dugout canoe, and continued walking all day.

At sunset, exhausted, we reached our destination, the house of a famous shaman, Akachu, deep in the forest. There was no *guayusa* that evening. Instead, I was proffered bowl after bowl of refreshing manioc beer, monkey meat, and raw, squirming, but delicious cheese-like grubs. Tired, but delighted to be back among shamans, I fell into a deep sleep on the bamboo bed.

In the morning Akachu and I sat formally, opposite each other on wooden stools, as his wives brought us bowls of warmed manioc beer. His long black hair, bound into a pony tail with a woven red and white strap from which a feathered tassel hung, showed streaks of gray. I guessed he was in his sixties.

"I have come," I explained, "to acquire spirit helpers, *tsentsak*."

He stared hard at me without saying a word, but the wrinkles in his brown face seemed to deepen.

"That is a fine gun, there," he observed, jutting his chin toward the Winchester shotgun I had brought along for hunting.

His message was clear, for the standard payment among the Jívaro for shamanic initiation was—at the very least—a muzzle-loading shotgun. The breach-loading, cartridge-using Winchester was far more powerful than the black-powder muzzle-loaders, and thus much more valuable.

"To acquire knowledge and spirit helpers, I will give you the gun and my two boxes of cartridges," I said.

Akachu nodded and reached his arm out in the direction of the Winchester. I picked up the gun and carried it over to him. He tested its weight and balance, and sighted along the barrel. Then, abruptly, he laid the gun across his knees.

"First, you must bathe in the waterfall," he said. "Then we will see."

I told him I was ready to do whatever he said.

"You are not a *shuar,* an Indian," Akachu said, "so I do not know if you will have success. But I will help you try." He pointed westward toward the Andes with his chin. "Soon we will make the journey to the waterfall."

Five days later, Akachu, his son-in-law Tsangu, and I departed on the pilgrimage to the sacred waterfall. My Jívaro guide, his duties finished, had already gone home.

The first day we followed a forest trail upstream along a twisting river valley. My companions kept up a very fast pace, and I was thankful when we at last stopped in late afternoon, beside a small rapid in the river. Akachu and Tsangu constructed a palm-thatched leanto, with a layer of palm fronds for our bed. I slept soundly, kept warm by the slow fire they built in the entrance of the shelter.

The second day our journey was almost a continuous climb upward into the mist-shrouded forest. As the virtually nonexistent trail became more difficult, we paused at a grove of *caña brava* to cut hiking staffs to help us in the ascent. Akachu briefly went off and returned with a three-inch thick pole of balsa wood. While we rested, he quickly carved it with simple geometric designs and then handed it to me.

"This is your magical staff," he said. "It will protect you from demons. If you encounter one, throw it at him. It is more powerful than a gun."

I fingered the pole. It was extremely light and obviously would be of no use in defending oneself against anything material. For a moment I felt as though we were children playing a game of make-believe. Yet these men were warriors, warriors who engaged in repeated life-and-death feuds and wars with their enemies. Didn't their survival depend upon being in genuine contact with reality?

As the day progressed, the trail became steeper and more slippery. Often it seemed that I was sliding one step back in the adobe-like mud for every two steps I made forward. We frequently rested to catch our breath and to sip water mixed with the manioc beer mash in our bottle-gourd canteens. Sometimes the others would snack on the smoked boiled manioc or smoked meat that they carried in their monkey-skin pouches. I, however, was forbidden to eat solid food.

"You must suffer," Tsangu explained, "so that the grandfathers will take pity on you. Otherwise, the ancient specter will not come."

That night, tired and hungry, I attempted to sleep in the palm-thatched leanto my companions had constructed for us on the top of a cold, dank ridge. Shortly before dawn, it began to rain. Too chilled and miserable to stay where we were, we broke camp and groped in the dark along the ridge. The rain grew in intensity. Soon bolts of lightning, accompanied by explosions of thunder, periodically illuminated our way. Many of the lightning strikes seemed to be on the very ridge we were following, so we began to move at maximum speed in order to get off

11

the heights. In the semi-darkness of the obscured dawn I often lost sight of the other two, who were much more accustomed to the incredible pace they were setting through the forest. Even under normal circumstances, the Indians loped along at about four or five miles an hour. Now it seemed like six.

Soon I lost sight of my companions entirely. I assumed they thought that I could follow them. They would undoubtedly be waiting for me somewhere ahead, beyond the end of the ridge. So I forged ahead, wet, tired, hungry, and fearful of being permanently lost in this great, uninhabited forest. One, two, three hours passed and I still did not encounter them. The rain let up and the light in the deserted forest grew stronger. I looked for the sharply bent branches of saplings, the Indians' sign that they had passed that way. But without luck.

I stopped, sat on a log in the middle of the dripping forest and tried to think clearly about my position. I gave the Indians' special long-distance yell, a cry from the depths of the lungs that can be heard a half-mile away. Three times I gave it. There was no answer. I was near panic. I did not have my gun, so hunting was impossible. I did not know where to go. The only humans that I knew of in the forest were my absent companions.

I was aware that we had been headed generally west, but the dense forest canopy prevented me from seeing the direction of the sun. The ridge had numerous forks, so that I could not tell which one would be the best to follow. Almost at random, I picked one ridge and followed it slowly, breaking branches every ten feet or so to guide my companions if they came searching that way. From time to time I yelled, but heard no answering sound. I stopped at a stream and added some water to the concentrated beer in my calabash. As I rested, sweating, dozens of butterflies swirled about, often settling on my head, shoulders and arms. I watched as they sucked the sweat from my skin and simultaneously urinated on it. I got up and went onward into the forest, supporting myself with the balsa staff. It was getting dark. With my·*puñal,* or short machete, I cut branches from palm saplings and made a crude lean-to. Exhausted, I drank some beer, covered my body with fronds, and soon fell asleep.

Faint light was filtering down through the forest canopy when I awoke. As I lay there in the green stillness, I heard a muffled boom. It caught me by surprise and I could not ascertain its direction. I quietly listened for perhaps fifteen minutes when another occurred, off to my left. It was clearly a gun. I jumped up and rushed off in the direction of the sound, running, stumbling, slipping as I skidded down steep slopes. From time to time I gave the long-distance yell. Another boom, this time slightly to my right. I veered course and soon found myself climbing down a preciptious canyon, clinging to vines and slipping from one sapling to another. I became aware of a pervasive roar, like a never-ceasing freight train. Abruptly, I was on the boulder-strewn shore of a river. About a quarter-mile upstream, a stupendous waterfall was hurtling over a bare rock cliff. And near its base I could see my companions; at that moment they were my closest friends in all the world.

I had to clamber up and down immense river boulders and ford the pools of water that lay between sandbars. As I got near, I felt the mists of the waterfall, carried down the canyon on the wind, cooling my face and arms. It took me about fifteen minutes to reach Akachu and Tsangu. Finally, I collapsed on the sand beside my companions.

"We thought a demon might have gotten you," said Akachu with a grin. I smiled back weakly, glad to accept the canteen of beer he offered.

"You are tired," he said. "That is good, for the grandfathers may take pity on you. You must now start to bathe."

He pointed to my staff. "Bring your balsa and come with me." While Tsangu sat on the sandbar, Akachu led me over the rocks along the edge of the great pool into which the cascade poured. Soon we were up against the wet cliff face, as drenching sprays pelted our bodies. He took my hand and inched forward along the base of the cliff. The water poured with mounting strength upon us, making it difficult to avoid being swept away. I supported myself with my staff with one hand and hung onto Akachu with the other.

Each step forward became more difficult. Then suddenly we were underneath the waterfall in a dark, natural recess. It seemed like a magical cave. Light entered only through the immense sheet of falling water, which sealed us in from the rest of the world. The incessant roar of the cascade was greater than even that of my first vision, years before. It seemed to penetrate my whole being. We were sealed from the world by the basic elements of earth and water.

"The House of the Grandfathers," Akachu shouted in my ear. He pointed to my staff.

He had told me earlier what to do. I began to walk back and forth in the incredible chamber, putting my staff before me with each step. As instructed, I continuously shouted, "Tau, tau, tau," to attract the

13

attention of the grandfathers. I was thoroughly chilled from the spray that swept the small cave, water which not long before had been reposing in the glacial lakes of the highest Andes. I shivered, paced, and shouted. Akachu accompanied me, but without a staff.

Gradually, a strange calm pervaded my consciousness. I no longer felt cold, tired, or hungry. The sound of the cascading water grew more and more distant and seemed strangely soothing. I felt that this was where I belonged, that I had come home. The wall of falling water became iridescent, a torrent of millions of liquid prisms. As they went by I had the continuous sensation of floating upward, as though they were stable and I was the one in motion. Flying inside of a mountain! I laughed at the absurdity of the world.

Finally, Akachu grasped my shoulder, stopped me, and took my hand. He led me out of the magic mountain, back along the cliff and to Tsangu. I was sorry to leave the sacred place.

When we had regrouped on the sandbar, Tsangu led us directly to the side of the canyon and commenced scaling the steep slope. We followed, single file, grasping at projecting roots, saplings, and vines to keep ourselves from sliding backward in the wet clay. For perhaps an hour we continued the arduous ascent, occasionally drenched by the wafting spray from the waterfall. It was late afternoon when we finally reached a small, flat ridge adjacent to the rim of the cascade. We rested briefly and then followed Tsangu along the plateau. At first the jungle growth was thick and difficult to penetrate, but shortly we found ourselves in a gallery of immense trees.

After about five minutes Tsangu stopped, and started to cut boughs for a lean-to.

Akachu began splitting a stick at one end. He split the same end a second time, at a right angle to the first cut, and stuck the unsplit end into the ground. Into the cross-wise split he pushed two twigs, which forced the end open into a four-pronged receptacle. Then he took a fist-sized gourd cup from his monkey-skin shoulder bag and set it into the space formed by the prongs. He reached again into his pouch and brought forth a bundle of short green stems. They were the *maikua* (a *Brugmansia* species of datura) plant cuttings he had collected prior to our departure from his house. One by one he held the stems over the gourd cup and scraped off the green bark. When he had finished, the cup was almost full. He reached in, drew out the shavings, and began squeezing their green juice into the cup. Within five minutes there was about an eighth of a cup of the liquid. He threw away the shavings.

14

"Now we will let the *maikua* cool," he said. "When night comes you will drink it. You alone will drink, for we must guard you. We will be with you at all times, so do not fear."

Tsangu had joined us, and now he added, "What is most important is that you must have no fear. If you see something frightening, you must not flee. You must run up and touch it."

Akachu grasped my shoulder. "That is right. You must do that or one day soon you will die. Hold your balsa at all times in your hands so that you can do the touching."

I began to feel a strong sense of panic. Not only were their words somewhat less than comforting, but I had heard that persons sometimes died or permanently lost their minds from taking *maikua*. I also remembered stories of Jívaro who had taken *maikua* and become so delirious that they had dashed wildly through the forest to fall from cliffs or to drown. For this reason, they never took *maikua* without sober companions to restrain them.[2]

"Will you hold me down strongly?" I asked.

"That will be done, brother," said Akachu.

It was the first time he had addressed me by a kinship term, and that one word reassured me. Still, as I waited for the dark, rising anticipation and curiosity were mixed with fear.

My companions did not make a fire, and as night came we were all stretched out side by side on palm fronds, listening to the stillness of the forest and the distant roar of the waterfall. At last the time came.

Akachu gave me the gourd cup. I tipped it up and swallowed the contents. The taste was somewhat disagreeable, yet slightly similar to green tomatoes. I felt a numbing sensation. I thought of that other drink, three years before among the Conibo, which had led me here. Was my shamanic quest worth the danger?

Shortly, however, even quasi-logical thought vanished as an inexpressible terror rapidly permeated my whole body. My companions were going to kill me! I must get away! I attempted to jump up, but instantly they were upon me. Three, four, an infinity of savages wrestled with me, forced me down, down, down. Their faces were above me, contorted into sly grins. Then blackness.

I was awakened by a flash of lightning followed by a thunderous explosion. The ground beneath me was shaking. I jumped up, utterly in a panic. A hurricane-like wind threw me back down on the ground. I stumbled again to my feet. A stinging rain pelted my body as the wind ripped at my clothes. Lightning and thunder exploded all around. I

15

grasped a sapling to support myself. My companions were nowhere to be seen.

Suddenly, about two hundred feet away amidst the tree trunks, I could see a luminous form floating slowly toward me. I watched, terrified, as it grew larger and larger, resolving itself into a twisting form. The gigantic, writhing reptilian form floated directly toward me. Its body shone in brilliant hues of greens, purples, and reds, and as it twisted amidst the lightning and thunder it looked at me with a strange sardonic smile.

I turned to run, and then remembered the balsa staff. I looked down but could not see it. The serpentine creature was now only twenty feet away and towering above me, coiling and uncoiling. It separated into two overlapping creatures. They were now both facing me. The dragons had come to take me away! They coalesced back into one. I saw before me a stick about a foot long. I grabbed it, and desperately charged the monster with my stick outstretched before me. An earsplitting scream filled the air, and abruptly the forest was empty. The monster was gone. There was only silence and serenity.

I lost consciousness.

When I awoke it was midday. Akachu and Tsangu were squatting beside a small fire, eating and conversing quietly. My head ached and I was hungry, but otherwise I felt all right. As I sat up, my friends rose and came over. Akachu gave me a bowl of warmed beer. I was also given a piece of dried monkey meat. The food tasted wonderful, but I wanted to share my experience with my friends.

I said, "I thought you were trying to kill me last night. Then you disappeared and there was tremendous lightning . . ."

Akachu interrupted me. "You must not tell anyone, even us, what you have encountered. Otherwise, all your suffering will have been in vain. Someday, and you will know when that is, you can tell others, but not now. Eat, and then we will start for home."

We went back to Akachu's house, and with his guidance I began to acquire the *tsentsak* (magical darts) essential to the practice of Jívaro shamanism. These *tsentsak* or spirit helpers are the main powers believed to cause and cure illness in daily life. To the nonshaman they are normally invisible, and even shamans can perceive them only in an altered state of consciousness.[3]

"Bad" or bewitching shamans send these spirit helpers into victims' bodies to make them ill or to kill them. "Good" shamans, or healers,

16

use their own *tsentsak* to help them suck out spirits from the bodies of ill tribesmen. The spirit helpers also form shields which, along with the shaman's guardian spirit power, protect their shaman masters from attacks.

A new shaman collects all kinds of insects, plants, and other objects, which become his spirit helpers. Almost any object, including living insects and worms, can become a *tsentsak* if it is small enough to be swallowed by a shaman. Different types of *tsentsak* cause, and are used to cure, different kinds of degrees of illness. The greater the variety of these power objects that a shaman has in his body, the greater is his ability as a doctor.

Each *tsentsak* has an ordinary and nonordinary aspect. The magical dart's ordinary aspect is an ordinary material object, as seen without drinking *ayahuasca*. But the nonordinary and "true" aspect of the *tsentsak* is revealed to the shaman by taking the drink. When he does this, the magical darts appear in their hidden forms as spirit helpers, such as giant butterflies, jaguars, serpents, birds, and monkeys, who actively assist the shaman in his tasks.

When a healing shaman is called in to treat a patient, his first task is diagnosis. He drinks *ayahuasca,* green tobacco water, and sometimes the juice of a plant called *piripiri,* in the late afternoon and early evening. The consciousness-changing substances permit him to see into the body of the patient as though it were glass. If the illness is due to sorcery, the healing shaman will see the intruding nonordinary entity within the patient's body clearly enough to determine whether he possesses the appropriate spirit helper to extract it by sucking.

A shaman sucks magical darts from a patient's body at night, and in a dark area of the house, for it is only in the darkness that he can perceive nonordinary reality. With the setting of the sun, he alerts his *tsentsak* by whistling the tune of his power song; after about a quarter of an hour, he starts singing. When he is ready to suck, the shaman keeps two *tsentsak,* of the type identical to the one he has seen in the patient's body, in the front and rear of his mouth. They are present in both their material and nonmaterial aspects, and are there to catch the nonordinary aspect of the magical dart when the shaman sucks it out of the patient's body. The *tsentsak* nearest the shaman's lips has the task of incorporating the sucked-out essence within itself. If, however, this nonordinary essence should get past it, the second spirit helper in the mouth blocks the throat so that the intruder cannot enter the interior of the shaman's body and do him harm. Trapped thus within the mouth,

17

the essence is shortly caught by, and incorporated into, the material substance of one of the curing shaman's *tsentsak*. He then "vomits" out this object and displays it to the patient and his family saying, "Now I have sucked it out. Here it is."

The nonshamans may think that the material object itself is what has been sucked out, and the shaman does not disillusion them. At the same time he is not lying, because he knows that the only important aspect of a *tsentsak* is its nonmaterial or nonordinary aspect, or essence, which he sincerely believes he has removed from the patient's body. To explain to the layman that he already had these objects in his mouth would serve no fruitful purpose and would prevent him from displaying such an object as proof that he had effected the cure.

The ability of the shaman to suck depends largely upon the quantity and strength of his own *tsentsak*, of which he may have hundreds. His magical darts assume their supernatural aspect as spirit helpers when he is under the influence of *ayahuasca*, and he sees them as a variety of zoomorphic forms hovering over him, perching on his shoulders, and sticking out of his skin. He sees them helping to suck the patient's body. He drinks tobacco water every few hours to "keep them fed" so that they will not leave him.

A healing shaman may have *tsentsak* sent at him by a bewitcher. Because of this danger, shamans may repeatedly drink tobacco water at all hours of the day and night. The tobacco water helps keep one's *tsentsak* ready to repel any other magical darts. A shaman does not even go for a walk without taking along the green tobacco leaves with which he prepares the water that keeps his spirit helpers alert.

The degree of violence and competition in Jívaro society is famous in the anthropological literature and contrasts radically, for example, with the peacefulness of the Conibo. And both the Jívaro and the Conibo stand apart from Australian and many other tribal peoples who have long practiced shamanism without employing psychedelics. Still Jívaro shamanism is highly developed, dramatic, and exciting. So in 1969 I again returned, filling in gaps in my knowledge, and in 1973 I engaged in more shamanic practice with them.

During the years since beginning shamanic work among the Conibo, I have also studied briefly with shamans of a few western North American Indian groups: the Wintun and Pomo in California, Coast Salish in Washington State, and the Lakota Sioux in South Dakota. From them I learned how shamanism could be practiced successfully without the use of the *ayahuasca* or other drugs of the

Conibo and the Jívaro. This knowledge has been especially useful in introducing Westerners to the practice of shamanism. Finally, I learned from the worldwide ethnographic literature on shamanism, where lie buried many gems of information that supplement and reaffirm what I had been taught firsthand. Now it seems time to help transmit some practical aspects of this ancient human legacy to those who have been cut off from it for centuries.

CHAPTER 2

The Shamanic Journey: Introduction

Shaman (pronounced SHAH-maan) is a word from the language of the Tungus people of Siberia, and has been adopted widely by anthropologists to refer to persons in a great variety of non-Western cultures who were previously known by such terms as "witch," "witch-doctor," "medicine man," "sorcerer," "wizard," "magic man," "magician," and "seer." One of the advantages of using the term is that it lacks the prejudicial overtones and conflicting meanings associated with the more familiar labels. Furthermore, not every kind of medicine man or witch doctor is a shaman.

A shaman is a man or woman who enters an altered state of consciousness—at will—to contact and utilize an ordinarily hidden reality in order to acquire knowledge, power, and to help other persons. The shaman has at least one, and usually more, "spirits" in his personal service.*

As Mircea Eliade observes, the shaman is distinguished from other kinds of magicians and medicine men by his use of a state of consciousness which Eliade, following Western mystical tradition, calls "ecstasy." But the practice of ecstasy alone, he properly emphasizes,

---

* For simplicity, I shall hereafter use the male pronominal form in referring to the shaman or the patient, with the clear understanding that shamans and patients may be of either gender.

does not define the shaman, for the shaman has specific techniques of ecstasy. Thus Eliade says: "Hence any ecstatic cannot be considered a shaman; the shaman specializes in a trance during which his soul is believed to leave his body and ascend to the sky or descend to the underworld."[1] To this I would add that, in his trance, he commonly works to heal a patient by restoring beneficial or vital power, or by extracting harmful power. The journey to which Eliade refers is especially undertaken to restore power or a lost soul.

The "ecstatic" or altered state of consciousness and the learned perspective that characterize shamanic work may be usefully termed the Shamanic State of Consciousness (hereafter referred to as the SSC). The SSC involves not only a "trance" or a transcendent state of awareness, but also a learned awareness of shamanic methods and assumptions while in such an altered state. The SSC contrasts with the Ordinary State of Consciousness (OSC), to which the shaman returns after engaging in his distinctive work. The SSC is the cognitive condition in which one perceives the "nonordinary reality" of Carlos Castaneda, and the "extraordinary manifestations of reality" of Robert Lowie.[2]

The learned component of the SSC includes information about the cosmic geography of nonordinary reality, so that one may know where to journey to find the appropriate animal, plant, and other powers. This includes knowledge of how the SSC provides access to the shamanic Lowerworld.

This knowledge includes an awareness by the shaman that he must have a specific intended mission while in the SSC. Nonordinary reality is entered not for play but for serious purposes. The shaman is a person with work to do in the SSC, and he must know the basic methods for accomplishing that work. If, for example, he wishes to recover a patient's guardian power animal from the Lowerworld, he must know the technique for reaching the Lowerworld, entering it, finding the power animal, and bringing it back safely. Subsequently, in the OSC, he must know what instructions to give the patient.

In the SSC, the shaman typically experiences an ineffable joy in what he sees, an awe of the beautiful and mysterious worlds that open before him. His experiences are like dreams, but waking ones that feel real and in which he can control his actions and direct his adventures. While in the SSC, he is often amazed by the reality of that which is presented. He gains access to a whole new, and yet familiarly ancient universe that provides him with profound information about the

21

meaning of his own life and death and his place within the totality of all existence. During his great adventures in the SSC, he maintains conscious control over the direction of his travels, but does not know what he will discover. He is a self-reliant explorer of the endless mansions of a magnificent hidden universe. Finally, he brings back his discoveries to build his knowledge and to help others.

The shaman is an accomplished see-er who works typically in the dark, or at least with the eyes covered, in order to see clearly. For this reason, shamans usually engage in their practices at night. Some kinds of shamanic seeing can be done with the eyes open, but usually that kind of perception is of a less profound nature. In darkness the distractions of ordinary reality lessen their impingement on consciousness, making it possible for the shaman to focus on the aspects of nonordinary reality essential to his work. But darkness alone is not enough for shamanic seeing. The seer must also enter the SSC, often assisted by drumming, rattling, singing, and dancing.

Shamanic enlightenment is the literal ability to lighten the darkness, to *see* in that darkness what others cannot perceive. This may, in fact, be the most ancient meaning of "enlightenment." For example, the special ability of the Iglulik Eskimo shaman to *see* is called his *qaumanEq*, his "lighting" or "enlightenment," ". . . which enables him to see in the dark, both literally and metaphorically speaking, for he can now, even with closed eyes, see through darkness and perceive things and coming events which are hidden from others; thus they look into the future and into the secrets of others."[3]

Aua, an Iglulik Eskimo shaman, described his shamanic enlightenment thus:

> . . . I endeavored to become a shaman by the help of others; but in this I did not succeed. I visited many famous shamans, and gave them great gifts. . . . I sought solitude, and here I soon became very melancholy. I would sometimes fall to weeping, and feel unhappy without knowing why. Then, for no reason, all would suddenly be changed, and I felt a great, inexplicable joy, a joy so powerful that I could not restrain it, but had to break into song, a mighty song, with only room for the one word: joy, joy! And I had to use the full strength of my voice. And then in the midst of such a fit of mysterious and overwhelming delight I became a shaman, not knowing myself how it came about. But I was a shaman. I could see and hear in a totally different way. I had gained my qaumanEq, my enlightenment, the shaman-light of brain and body, and this in such a manner that it was not only I who could see through the darkness of life,

22

but the same light also shone out from me, imperceptible to human beings, but visible to all the spirits of earth and sky and sea, and these now came to me and became my helping spirits.[4]

Among the Wiradjeri of Australia, the shamanic neophyte becomes "enlightened" by being sprinkled with a "sacred powerful water" that is considered liquefied quartz. Eliade observes, "All this is as much as to say that one becomes a shaman when one is stuffed with 'solidified light,' that is, with quartz crystals. . . ." He suggests, "they feel a relation between the condition of a supernatural being and a superabundance of light."[5]

The perception of the shaman as one who is giving off light, particularly in a "crown," an aura from the head, is also true of the Jívaro. The halo, which is multicolored, forms only when the shaman is in an *ayahuasca*-induced altered state of consciousness. It can only be seen by another shaman in a similar state of consciousness (see Plate 1).

Plate 1.   Golden halo around the head of a Jívaro shaman in an altered state of consciousness. Drawn by another Jívaro shaman.

At the same time that the Jívaro shaman is radiating light, he is able to see into the darkness and even through ordinarily opaque material. As I have described it elsewhere:

> He had drunk, and now he softly sang. Gradually, faint lines and forms began to appear in the darkness, and the shrill music of the *tsentsak,* the spirit helpers, arose around him. The power of the drink fed them. He called, and they came. First, *pangi,* the anaconda, coiled about his head, transmuted into a crown of gold. Then *wampang,* the giant butterfly, hovered above his shoulder and sang to him with its wings. Snakes, spiders, birds, and bats danced in the air above him. On his arms appeared a thousand eyes as his demon helpers emerged to search the night for enemies.
>
> The sound of rushing water filled his ears, and listening to its roar, he knew he possessed the power of *Tsungi,* the first shaman. Now he could see.[6]

Shamans often work in a house plunged into total darkness, or they may allow a small fire or lamp to burn; but sometimes even a small amount of light can interfere with the shamanic seeing. Thus, among the Chukchee of Siberia, the shamanic session:

> . . . began, as usual, in the dark; but when the shaman suddenly broke off beating the drum, the lamp was again lighted and the face of the shaman immediately covered with a piece of cloth. The mistress of the house, who was the wife of the shaman, took up the drum and began to beat it with light, slow strokes. This lasted the entire time. . . .[7]

Personally, I usually leave a candle burning somewhere on the floor of the dark room when entering the SSC and then, when I lie or drop down on the floor, I simply cover my closed eyes with my left forearm to exclude all light.

When the shaman either slowly or suddenly drops to the dirt floor of the house, the Chukchee say "he sinks," which refers not only to his material act, visible to the others in the house, but also to "the belief that the shaman, during the period of ecstasy, is able to visit other worlds, and especially that underground."[8] In a related fashion, the Eskimo shaman about to make the journey is referred to as "one who drops down to the bottom of the sea."[9] He not only drops to the floor of the house (OSC), but drops into an oceanic Lowerworld (SSC).

The shamanic journey is one of the most important tasks to be undertaken. The basic form of this journey, and the one usually easiest to learn, is the journey to the Lowerworld. To undertake this, a shaman

24

typically has a special hole or entrance into the Lowerworld. This entrance exists in ordinary reality as well as in nonordinary reality. The entrance among California Indian shamans, for example, frequently was a spring, especially a hot spring. Shamans were reputed to travel hundreds of miles underground, entering one hot spring and coming out at another. Australian shamans of the Chepara tribe were similarly believed to dive into the ground and come out again where they liked, and those of Fraser Island were said "to go into the earth and come out again at a considerable distance."[10] Similarly, a !Kung Bushman shaman in the Kalahari desert of southern Africa recounted:

> My friend, that's the way of this n/um [power]. When people sing, I dance. I enter the earth. I go in at a place like a place where people drink water [a waterhole]. I travel in a long way, very far.[11]

Another entrance used by California Indians was a hollow tree stump. Among the Arunta (Aranda) of Australia a hollow tree was an entrance to the Underworld.[12] The Conibo Indians taught me to follow the roots of the giant *catahua* tree down into the ground to reach the Lowerworld. In the SSC, the roots were transformed for me and my Conibo friends into black serpents down whose backs we slid to reach lands of forests, lakes, and rivers, and strange cities bright as day, lit by a sun that had disappeared from the ordinary world above—for these journeys were taken at night.

Other shamans' entrances into the Lowerworld include caves, holes of burrowing animals, and even special holes in the dirt floor of houses. Among the Twana of the Northwest Coast of North America, for example, the surface of the earth floor was reportedly often physically broken open for the descent.[13]

Entrances into the Lowerworld commonly lead down into a tunnel or tube that conveys the shaman to an exit, which opens out upon bright and marvelous landscapes. From there the shaman travels wherever he desires for minutes or even hours, finally returning back up through the tube (henceforth called the Tunnel) to emerge at the surface, where he entered. A fine description of a shaman using this classic and widespread method is given by Rasmussen for the Iglulik Eskimo of Hudson Bay:

> . . . For the very greatest [shamans], a way opens right from the house whence they invoke their helping spirits; a road down through the earth, if they are in a tent on shore, or down through the sea, if it is in a snow hut on the sea ice, and by this route the shaman is led down without

encountering any obstacle. He almost glides as if falling through a tube so fitted to his body that he can check his progress by pressing against the sides, and need not actually fall down with a rush. This tube is kept open for him by all the souls of his namesakes, until he returns on his way back to earth.[14]

When the Eskimo shaman returns from his journey to the Lowerworld, the people in the tent or igloo "can hear him coming a long way off; the rush of his passage through the tube kept open for him by his spirits comes nearer and nearer, and with a mighty 'Plu—a—he—he' he shoots up into his place behind the curtain."[15]

Most of us who are engaged in shamanic work do not find the Tunnel at all constricting. Usually it is spacious and provides ample room for movement. Sometimes obstacles in the Tunnel may obstruct the passage, but one normally can find a crack or opening to go through. With patience, one usually succeeds in passing through it without having to give up the journey and return home.

Sometimes, when the shaman enters down through the hole, he finds himself ascending or descending a stream or river which may or may not be clearly part of the Tunnel. Thus a Tavgi Samoyed shaman, recounting his first journey through the entrance to the Lowerworld, said:

> As I looked around, I noticed a hole in the earth. . . . The hole became larger and larger. We [he and his guardian spirit companion] descended through it and arrived at a river with two streams flowing in opposite directions. "Well, find out this one too!" said my companion, "one stream goes from the centre to the north, the other to the south—the sunny side."[16]

Outstanding shamans not only see in the SSC, but hear, feel, and even experience communications or sensations beyond the usual senses. Thus this Samoyed shaman heard his guardian spirit, and thus a Pomo Indian woman shaman in California told me how she felt a gigantic power animal move under her as she traveled inside a mountain through the Tunnel.[17]

Among the Bellacoola Indians of the Northwest Coast, each house reportedly had a hole in the earth floor which was used as the entrance into the Lowerworld:

> The world below us is . . . called Asiutā´nEm. Descriptions of the [Lowerworld] are principally obtained from shamans who believe they

have visited that country during a trance. According to the statement of an old woman who believed that as a little girl she had visited the [Lowerworld] during a trance, the entrance . . . is through a hole situated in each house, between the doorway and the fireplace.[18]

In a remarkably similar fashion, the entrance to the Underworld in the circular *kivas* (ceremonial chambers) of the Zuni Indians in the American Southwest is a hole located in the floor. The main contrast with the Bellacoola is that the hole, called a *sipapu,* is in the floor between the fireplace and the wall (the doorway is in the roof).[19] Such *sipapu* holes were common in prehistoric *kivas* of the Puebloan peoples, but absent from those of some of the present-day Pueblos. Interestingly, at Zuni, where the *sipapu* survives in the circular form of *kiva,* so do the shamanistic medicine societies.[20] Although I have no hard evidence, I would not be surprised if the members of the medicine societies at Zuni used the holes to enter the Lowerworld when in trance. The orthodox ethnological view, however, is that the kiva *sipapu* is merely "a symbol representing the mythical opening into the underworld through which the ancestors are supposed to have reached the world."[21] The Puebloan Hopi, unlike the Zuni, do not have *sipapu* in the floors of their kivas.[22] However, they believe a peculiar rock formation located some distance from them, which has a hole in its top, is the original *sipapu,* or entrance into the Lowerworld (see Plate 2). That the Hopi

Plate 2. Sepapu [sipapu]. *Entrance to the Hopi Lowerworld. Located in the Grand Canyon west of the Hopi villages. Source: Center of Astrogeology, U.S. Geological Survey.*

27

may use it in shamanistic visualizations for journeys to the Lowerworld is an unproven, but distinct possibility. Since medicine society work is highly secret among the Puebloan peoples, non-Hopis may never know for certain. A recent painting by a Hopi artist, titled *"Se Pa Po Nah"* [*sipapu-nah*] is highly suggestive, however, of the mandala-like Tunnel experience (see Plate 3).

Incidentally, the concentric circles of a mandala often resemble the ribbed aspect that the Tunnel frequently presents, and meditation with the mandala can lead to an experience resembling the entrance into the Tunnel. As Joan M. Vastokas has perceptively observed in her discussion of certain aspects of shamanic art, "... the concentric motif

Plate 3. Se Pa Po Nah [sipapu-nah]. *Contemporary painting by the Hopi artist Milland Lomakema* (Dawakema). *Source:* Hopi Painting: The World of the Hopis, *by Patricia Janis Broder. New York: Dutton, 1978.*

28

seems characteristic of the visionary experience itself and stands for the aperture through which the shaman penetrates the Underworld or Sky, by means of which he transcends the physical universe."[23]

Thus, as she points out, Alaskan Eskimo shamans' masks sometimes have the form of "concentric circles radiating from a central void." An example of one such mask, which bears a startling resemblance to the ribbed Tunnel, may be seen in Plate 4. Similarly, in Tibetan Buddhism, which was heavily influenced by shamanism, a very complex mandala

Plate 4. Eskimo shaman's mask. Nineteenth century, from the Lower Yukon River. Source: National Museum of Natural History, Smithsonian Institution. Photo: Victor E. Krantz.

may have the tunnel-like circle only in the center to serve as the entrance place to the worlds of the gods and spirits represented around it (see the Tibetan tanka in Plate 5; also note its remarkable similarity to the painting by the Hopi artist of the entrance to the Lowerworld in Plate 3). With the aid of darkness and drumming, the shaman does not focus on a mandala, but moves directly into the Tunnel and then beyond.

First Journey

Now you are ready for your first experiential exercise in shamanism. This will be a simple journey of exploration down through the Tunnel

Plate 5. Mandala of Kunrig. Tibetan Buddhist tanka on cloth, ca. fifteenth century. Source: The Royal Ontario Museum.

into the Lowerworld. Your only mission will be to traverse the Tunnel, perhaps see what lies beyond, and then return. Make sure you thoroughly understand these instructions before you begin.

To carry out the exercise, you will need a drum (or a cassette recording of shamanic drumming) and someone to assist you by beating the drum.* If you do not possess a drum or stereo cassette player, you might have someone tap rapidly with a tablespoon on a hardcover book close to your head. This is only a stopgap technique, however, and normally is much less effective than drumming.

Wait until you are calm and relaxed before undertaking this or any other shamanic exercise. Avoid psychedelic or alcoholic substances during the preceding twenty-four hours, so that your centeredness and power of concentration will be good, and your mind clear of confusing imagery. Eat only lightly or not at all during the preceding four hours. Choose a dark and quiet room. Take off your shoes, loosen your clothing, and lie comfortably on the floor, without a pillow. Take a few deep breaths. Relax your arms and legs. Lie there a few minutes and contemplate your forthcoming mission. Then close your eyes, placing a hand or forearm over them to keep out any light.

Now visualize an opening into the earth that you remember from some time in your life. It can be an opening you remember from your childhood, or one you saw last week, or even today. Any kind of entry into the ground will do—it may be a hole made by a burrowing animal, a cave, a hollow tree stump, a spring, or even a swamp. It can even be a man-made opening. The right opening is one that really feels comfortable to you, and one which you can visualize. Spend a couple of minutes seeing the hole without going into it. Note its details clearly.

Now instruct your companion to start beating the drum in a strong, monotonous, unvarying, and rapid beat. There should be no contrast in intensity of the drum beats or in the intervals between them. A drumming tempo of about 205 to 220 beats per minute is usually effective for this journey. Allow yourself about ten minutes for the journey. Instruct your assistant to stop the drumming at the end of ten minutes, striking the drum sharply four times to signal to you that it is time to return. Then your assistant should immediately beat the drum very rapidly for about a half a minute to accompany you on the return journey, concluding with four more sharp strikes of the drum to signal that the journey is over.

When the drumming begins, visualize your familiar opening into the

* See Appendix A for information on drums and cassettes.

earth, enter it, and begin the journey. Go down through the opening and enter the Tunnel. At first the Tunnel may be dark and dim. It usually goes underground at a slight angle, but occasionally it descends steeply. The Tunnel sometimes appears ribbed, and often it bends. Occasionally one passes through the Tunnel so fast it is not even seen. In following the Tunnel you may run up against a natural wall of stone or some other obstacle. When this happens, just go around it or through a crack in it. If this fails, simply come back to try again. In any case, do not exert yourself too hard in making the journey. If you do this work correctly, it will be relatively effortless. Success in journeying and seeing depends on an attitude that lies between trying too hard and not trying hard enough.

At the end of the Tunnel you will emerge out of doors. Examine the landscape in detail, travel through it, and remember its features. Explore until you are signalled to come back, and then return up through the Tunnel the same way you went down. *Do not bring anything back with you.* This is only an exploratory journey.

When you have emerged, sit up and open your eyes. Do not be discouraged if you did not succeed the first time. Try it again, with the drumming at a slower or faster beat. Different persons require a different tempo on different occasions.

When you complete the exercise, describe to your companion what you saw so that you will not forget the details of the experience. You may also write them down or dictate them into a cassette recorder. The act of remembering these experiential details is the beginning of your accumulation of SSC knowledge.

Some of the people in my workshops have been kind enough to provide me with accounts of their experiences during this first exercise. You may find it instructive to compare your own experience with theirs. Here are a few of their accounts, prefaced by my comments. You will notice that they sometimes mention my calling them back from the journey. This is something I usually do in group sessions, simply to coordinate the participants.

Journeys

Following are firsthand accounts of the experiences of persons undertaking the journey into the Lowerworld for the first time, as related by them afterwards. The narrators are mainly middle-class Americans from a variety of backgrounds. In their descriptions, you may note the absence of any qualifying expressions such as, "I imagined that . . ." or "I fantasized that . . ." Carried along by the drum and using the simple method just described, they had experiences which they found to be real in a new way, and which they often described afterward as among the most profound in their lives. You should be able to have a comparable experience by using the simple method just outlined.

The first account provides an excellent description of the frequent concentric circle appearance of the walls of the Tunnel.

When the drum began to beat, I sought out in my mind places I had known which might provide the access I was looking for. I visualized a couple of places that had been important to me and which I thought might work . . . but neither seemed right; then there was a high cave at Pyramid Lake in Nevada, mysterious and with a grand view, but it seemed like an awfully long tunnel I would have to travel from up there; finally there was a majestic cave from my childhood, one of those tourist places; was it called "Ruby Cave"? It was somewhere in the South, maybe Georgia, or North Carolina.

Anyway, it was full of stalactites and stalagmites—a REAL cave. I moved off into a dark and narrow area and found, not the cave of my childhood fantasies with animals and dragons and beasts of every kind, but a new kind of cave. Concentric rings of light and dark opened up around me and seemed to carry me along them. It was not so much a sense that I was moving through the tunnel but that it was moving along me. At first the rings were circular, but they changed shape and became vertical ellipses, always concentric and always moving. The alternating patterns of dark and light were faintly reminiscent of a glow caught. between the ridges of a corrugated pipe.

From time to time I became impatient that the tunnel seemed to go on and on; then I would remind myself that, although it would be nice to experience whatever was beyond the tunnel, it was enough that I was experiencing the tunnel. The vertical ellipses shifted and gave way to horizontal ones which, after a time, opened up gradually along the horizontal axis and began to break up, giving way to a gray and dimly lit landscape—an underground sea—which I passed over for a long time, closely watching the waves rise, gather and move away beneath me.

The tunnel which brought me to this place had been at a slightly downward angle of perhaps fifteen degrees; but now the darkened sky over this underground sea directed me into another tunnel which took an immediate and downward turn of ninety degrees and I was again being carried through it, by it. Its walls were once again the by now familiar concentric circles of light and shade, almost pulsing me through; there

33

was no sense of falling but of quite *deliberate* movement.

I was surprised to hear myself being called back, and reluctantly I allowed myself to return, somewhat disappointed at not coming to the end of the tunnel and, at the same time, amazed at the experience. The return itself was quick and easy. The sense of discovery and of awe remains.

The second person also used a cave as an entrance into the earth, and noted having experienced a sleep-like state of consciousness.

I chose a cave that was familiar to me. I've been to it four or five times. It's in a wooded forest and the entrance is about four feet in diameter. You go down into a large room with several passages. It continues down into a mountain. I had to go over some crevices that were pretty deep, and there was one spot where I got to a place where you literally have to squirm your way through—very difficult to do it just by yourself.

I went on down, to the deepest part of the cave that I've been in. I had never really been any farther than that. But I just kind of went even further and came out at another entrance or, in this case, an exit, and I came out onto a tropical island with a nice big shore, just tropical birds and a lot of tropical vegetation. A run-of-the-mill paradise!

Then I came back. It was almost as if I had been sleeping, but I know myself well enough to know when I'm sleeping; and I wasn't sleeping.

The next case is another example of using a cave as the entrance:

I seemed to take a long time getting started. I finally focused in on a cave that I had visited in France where primitive people had lived. I walked in and kept walking and walking. It never seemed to get much smaller than maybe my height, so I didn't have to crawl. So I just kept walking along. Eventually it widened into a large opening. I walked out and there was a cliff. I walked around it and climbed up the hill so that I was sitting over the opening. I enjoyed the view, which was very deep and broad. Then I came back.

Persons with unusual shamanic potential may, even in this first experience, not only *see* but feel, hear, and smell in their experiences. In the following example, the person felt the sensation of climbing on hands and knees, the sensation of sliding, and the coldness of water, in addition to simply seeing.

I started out in a little spring that's on the property where I now live. I felt myself getting very small as I went under a big rock. I entered a tiny little wet channel and it went uphill for quite a while. I felt myself climbing on my hands and knees. It was very dark in there. It got very dark as soon as I couldn't see the opening any more. Then it started a very sudden descent and I didn't know where it was going. I felt myself sliding down on the wet rocks and ending up in a very big space where there was a pool of water. The water was very cold.

Across this water was a tiny light and I felt there must be something beyond or outside, so I went through the water and had to partly wade and partly swim. I remember the sensation of being very cold. Then it was a very steep climb up a little channel, like in a cave. I came out into a meadow that was very green and shaded by a huge oak tree. I sat down under the oak tree and discovered that I had leather clothes on, like Indian leggings and an Indian shirt.

I was feeling very comfortable under that tree when it was time to come back. I felt annoyed at having to come back, but being a good student, I followed the instructions and got to the area where I had to climb back out of the pool. I discovered I didn't have the leggings on any more, I just had blue jeans and my climbing boots. Then I came out into the little spring again. The sky was kind of gray, overcast. It felt like home, like I was back where I belonged.

In the case below, the journeyer not only felt a "cool, moist soil," but heard also the babbling of water, and felt the wind while standing on a hilltop in the Lowerworld.

I had a little bit of a problem getting started because, when you told us to choose an opening to enter, I had two images in my head. I tried out one first that was just a sort of a cave in the side of a hill that a bulldozer had chopped that way. I climbed up into the cave and it didn't go anywhere—I couldn't make it open up for me visually.

So I went to the other place, which is a hollow tree trunk on some property that belongs to a friend of mine—I was there maybe a month ago. So I crawled in there and went down through a small opening just barely big enough for me. I crawled through on my stomach. It wasn't an unpleasant feeling like mud, but just sort of a cool, moist soil. I could hear a babbling at one point. On this particular property I'm talking about there's a creek that runs over it. I could kind of hear water, like I was going under the creek. I crawled for a long distance and them came out on a hilltop.

I had really good feelings looking out from the top of the hill in all directions. As I was standing there I could feel the wind coming through behind me. It was kind of like the wind filled me up with a really nice feeling.

Then when you told us to come back I got back on the ground and started coming back. I got kind of anxious when the drum started getting faster, like my heart started beating faster, it was like I wasn't sure I was going to make it back in time. In fact, I was trying to get back, but it was a small opening. Then finally when you hit the drum the last time I had kind of a flash of light.

In the next example, the person not only had the experience of smelling, but found a new entrance underground through which to return to the surface.

I started off swimming in the ocean. Then I went into an enormous whirlpool, hundreds of feet across or more. It just spun me down and down and down and down. That lasted most of the journey. I kept thinking, how am I going to land safely? I finally broke through and I fell onto this enormous daisy. It was big enough to cushion my fall. It smelled pretty good. Then you said come back and I found a cave, a system of caves, and I just whooshed back up through them.

The following case illustrates how the person in the SSC learns new abilities, such as how to "swim through the earth." Thus occurs the experiential accumulation of shamanic knowledge as to how to do things that would be impossible in ordinary reality.

I went down to the bottom of a tunnel and then I came to water at the bottom. I was entering through the water but I had to play around there for a while to try and find the cracks in the rock, and I really couldn't see how to travel in the rock. But then I found if I spread my limbs out and made myself a little bit flatter I could swim through the earth.

Similarly, the shaman in the SSC learns how to metamorphose himself into other forms of matter, as happened in the following case. Note how this person, in the midst of such a radical transformation, was simultaneously aware of the existence of ordinary reality. This is common in shamanic work, with a small portion of one's consciousness remaining in the OSC to monitor ordinary reality and thereby to provide a bridge for a relatively rapid total return to the OSC.

I went through a clearing in the woods that I remember when I was very young. Going through, I was very aware of how small I was, how everything was so much bigger than I. It was as though I were in a tunnel.

36

I was very aware of sounds, the smell of the woods and my size.

I just got into a cave, but it was not too deep. I just all of a sudden dissolved myself, I became water to get into the cracks, just lying down. I was very much aware of what was going on here in the room also, hearing you beating the drum. So I was simultaneously in two realities. Then I came back the same way.

Occasionally in traversing the tunnel, one loses track of direction or gets "boxed in." This sometimes happens even to experienced Jívaro shamans. If you cannot find a way out, just relax and wait a while. You will come back effortlessly, even if somewhat slowly, as in the following case.

Once I saw these ground squirrels when I was camping, their holes were all over. So that's where I went down; through one of their holes. At first I started going through these small little tunnels. Then all of a sudden I reached a point where a tunnel was straight down and I started traveling real fast straight down. I couldn't see the end and it went on for quite a while. I just couldn't stop and I didn't know where I was going. It was all black. I got a little disoriented in there for a little bit. I didn't come back up as fast as I went down, but I eventually came up, although I didn't come back the same way.

Even an experienced shaman may be unsuccessful in penetrating an obstacle in his descent. Then there is simply nothing to do but return, as did this person:

I went down through a hot spring in the middle of a river. It kind of erupts from the bottom. I went down and I sort of visualized what it's like, no colors ar anything. Then I ended up at a sheet of lava or magma. I didn't know how to penetrate it so that I could travel along it. I was just stuck there and I didn't know what to do. Then you beat the drum for us to come back up and I returned.

Even on the first journey a person of unusual shamanic potential may encounter animal, plant, or even human forms, as in the next case. This particular person's potentialities are further suggested by the fact that he flew in his first experience. Note also how, like the Eskimo shaman referred to earlier, he had to struggle to pass down into the earth. Even for those with considerable potential, shamanic work is sometimes difficult.

37

I entered some large caverns that I know. I remembered there was an area they haven't explored yet, so I went down in there. It was very narrow for a long time, and I had to really squeeze and push to get through. Then it suddenly opened out into a really large area. It went for a long, long way and I was traveling, traveling, traveling. I realized that I had a long way to go, so suddenly I just started to fly.

I was just moving very quickly, flying all the way through. When I got to sort of the center, there were all these nature spirits, very ethereal-type bodies everywhere. At first they were just standing around and then they all started dancing to the beat of the drum. They were all going the same way at the same time and I was seeing different ones. There was a frog one that had big eyes and looked really strange, and a tree one that was very tall. They were all moving to the drum beat. Then I just returned when you said to come back.

Animals were encountered in the next case, too. This person encounters a "pterodactyl-bird," and with appropriate shamanic confidence senses that it is nothing of which to be frightened:

I went down an old abandoned mine shaft and when I got in there it turned dark. Somehow I couldn't really begin the journey. Then a platform appeared with wheels on it and it started taking me off down this shaft. Pretty soon the shaft got lighter and lighter, and very yellow. There were individual little chambers. Each one of the chambers had an animal in it, some type of prehistoric animal. Each was doing something, I don't know what they were doing, but they were moving in incredible agitation.

Then the platform began to slow down. The shaft was still yellow. As I turned to look at the animals, a thing came out of the wall like a red and black pterodactyl-bird. It was hooded and flapping its wings at me. I wasn't frightened; it seemed more playful than anything. Then you called us back. As you called us back, it acted as if it wanted me to stay there. The platform began moving back toward the opening, and I came back.

In our final example of a first journey, the person sensed that he had brought back a beneficial or beneficent entity. This is a classic kind of shamanic work that the person had simply stumbled on involuntarily in his first experience in the SSC. I asked him if he had already known what I did in my workshops, since that might account for his experience. He, however, replied, "No, I tried to find out something about the workshop and I never did." Presumably this person has considerable shamanic potential.

38

I started off in a spring. I jumped into the spring and followed the water through the tunnel. Then I came out where another spring was flowing out into a clearing on the side of a mountain. I was facing northwest—for some reason I knew it was northwest. I sat down with the spring on my left and the forest on my right. It felt perfect. No other place in the area felt right, but that spot felt perfect.

Then I came back. I just jumped into the spring and swam back to the opening where I began. The strange thing was that when I got back and had gotten out, I had the distinct impression that something had come back with me. It was right behind me. It was beneficial or benevolent; it was not bad.

CHAPTER 3

Shamanism and
States of Consciousness

Shamanism represents the most widespread and ancient methodological system of mind-body healing known to humanity. Archaeological and ethnological evidence suggests that shamanic methods are at least twenty or thirty thousand years old. Quite possibly, the methods have much greater antiquity—for, after all, primates that could be called human have been on the planet for more than two or three million years.

Today shamanic knowledge survives primarily among people who, until recently, had primitive cultures. The knowledge that they preserve was acquired over hundreds of human generations, in situations of life and death. The ancestors of these peoples painstakingly learned and used this knowledge in their efforts to maintain health and strength, to cope with serious illness, and to deal with the threat and trauma of death. These custodians of the ancient methods are very important to us, for almost none of their cultures left written records. Thus it is only from their remaining living representatives that we can learn the shamanic principles.

One of the remarkable things about shamanic assumptions and methods is that they are very similar in widely separated and remote parts of the planet, including such regions as aboriginal Australia, native North and South America, Siberia and central Asia, eastern and northernmost Europe, and southern Africa. Even in the historical literature from the Classical Mediterranean, or from medieval and Renaissance western Europe, one finds evidence that the same basic shamanic knowledge once existed there until it was largely eradicated by the Inquisition.

The widespread similarities in shamanic methods and beliefs throughout much of the world have been extensively documented by Eliade in his classic work, *Shamanism*.[1] It is precisely because of the consistency of this ancient power and healing system that Eliade and others can speak with confidence of the occurrence of shamanism among peoples long isolated from one another.[2] For example, one anthropologist notes: "Wherever shamanism is still encountered today, whether in Asia, Australia, Africa, or North and South America, the shaman functions fundamentally in much the same way and with similar techniques—as guardian of the psychic and ecological equilibrium of his group and its members, as intermediary between the seen and unseen worlds, as master of spirits, as supernatural curer, etc." The shaman is able "to transcend the human condition and pass freely back and forth through the different cosmological planes. . . ."[3]

The remarkable worldwide consistency in basic shamanic knowledge has also been noted by many other anthropologists. Wilbert, for instance, writing on the nature of shamanism among the Warao Indians of Venezuela, notes, "It will have been immediately apparent to anyone familiar with the literature on shamanism that the Warao experience contains much that is near-universal. . . ." He provides a long list of the practices and beliefs that the Warao shamans share with those elsewhere in Australia, Indonesia, Japan, China, Siberia, and native North America, Mexico, and South America. Wilbert further concludes that there is a "remarkable correspondence . . . not only in general content but specific detail" between the shamanic journeys of the Venezuelan Warao and the Wiradjeri of Australia, an ocean and continent away.[4]

The shamanic approach to power and healing was maintained in a basically similar form in primitive cultures that otherwise represented radically different adaptations to contrasting environments and to distinctly different problems of material survival. Through prehistoric migrations and isolation, many such groups were separated from other divisions of the human family for ten or twenty thousand years. Yet, through all those years, the basic shamanic knowledge did not seem to change significantly.

Why was this? It was obviously not due to lack of imagination on the part of primitive peoples, for there is great contrast and variation in their social systems, art, economics, and many other aspects of their cultures. Why, then, is shamanic knowledge so basically consistent in different parts of the primitive world?

I suggest that the answer is, simply, because it works. Over many thousands of years, through trial and error, people in ecological and cultural situations that were often extremely different came nonetheless to the same conclusions as to the basic principles and methods of shamanic power and healing.

Shamanism flourished in ancient cultures that lacked the technological innovations of modern medicine. In my opinion, the low technological level of those cultures compelled their members to develop to the highest degree possible the ability of the human mind to cope with serious problems of health and survival. Some of the most interesting methods that humans possess with regard to the health and healing potentialities of the mind are those of the shamans in these low-technology cultures.

To perform his work, the shaman depends on special, personal power, which is usually supplied by his guardian and helping spirits. Each shaman generally has at least one guardian spirit in his service, whether or not he also possesses helping spirits. In her classic work on the concept of the guardian spirit in native North America, Ruth F. Benedict observes, shamanism "is practically everywhere in some fashion or in some aspect built around the vision-guardian spirit complex. . . ."[5]

Outside of North America, the guardian spirit is similarly important, but is often called by other names in the anthropological literature, such as "tutelary spirit" in works on Siberian shamanism, and as "nagual" in Mexico and Guatemala. In the Australian literature it may be referred to as an "assistant totem," and in the European literature as a "familiar." Sometimes the guardian spirit is just called the "friend" or "companion." Whatever it is called, it is a fundamental source of power for the shaman's functioning.

The best-known way to acquire a guardian spirit is in a spirit quest in a remote place in the wilderness. The location may be a cave, the top of a mountain, or a tall waterfall or an isolated trail at night, as among the Jívaro. There are also involuntary as well as special shamanic ways to secure a guardian spirit.

Without a guardian spirit it is virtually impossible to be a shaman, for the shaman must have this strong, basic power source in order to cope with and master the nonordinary or spiritual powers whose existence and actions are normally hidden from humans. The guardian spirit is often a *power animal,* a spiritual being that not only protects and serves the shaman, but becomes another identity or alter ego for him.

The fact that a person has a guardian spirit does not in itself make him a shaman. As the Jívaro point out, whether an adult knows it or not, he probably has, or has had, the aid of a guardian spirit in his childhood; otherwise he would not have had the protective power necessary to achieve adulthood. The main difference between an ordinary person and a shaman with regard to their guardian spirits is that the shaman uses his guardian spirit actively when in an altered state of consciousness. The shaman frequently sees and consults with his guardian spirit, travels with it on the shamanic journey, has it help him, and uses it to help others to recover from illness and injury.

In addition to the guardian spirit, a powerful shaman normally has a number of spirit helpers. These are individually minor powers, compared to the guardian spirit, but there may be hundreds of them at a particular shaman's disposal, providing great collective power. These helping spirits have specialized functions for particular purposes. It usually takes years for a shaman to accumulate a large crew of them.

There does not seem to be any obvious difference between the sexes in terms of shamanic aptitude and potentiality. In many societies, such as that of the Jívaro, for economic and social reasons that have little connection with the practice of shamanism itself, most of the shamans are men. But even Jívaro women, after they have finished raising their children and reach middle age, sometimes become shamans, indeed very powerful ones. In medieval and Renaissance Europe, widows and elderly women similarly often became healing shamans, partly to support themselves. Of course, the Inquisition termed them "witches," as Christian missionaries commonly still call shamans in non-Western societies.

Shamans are especially healers, but they also engage in divination, seeing into the present, past, and future for other members of the community. A shaman is a *see-er.* Our word "seer" refers to this kind

43

of activity, a survival of our almost vanished European shamanic heritage. A shaman may also engage in clairvoyance, seeing what is going on elsewhere at the present moment.

The shaman moves between realities, a magical athlete of states of consciousness engaged in mythic feats. The shaman is a middle man between ordinary reality and nonordinary reality, as Castaneda has dramatically described. The shaman is also a "power-broker" in the sense of manipulating spiritual power to help people, to put them into a healthy equilibrium.

A shaman may be called upon to help someone who is *dis-spirited,* that is, who has lost his personal guardian spirit or even his soul. In such cases, the shaman undertakes a healing journey in nonordinary reality to recover the lost spirit or soul and return it to the patient. Or a shaman's patient may be suffering from a localized pain or illness. In such a case, the shaman's task is to extract the harmful power to help restore the patient to health. These are the two basic approaches to shamanic healing: restoring beneficial powers and taking out harmful ones.

Shamans have to be able to journey back and forth between realities in these healing tasks. To do this, in some cultures, shamans take mind-altering substances; but in many other cultures they do not.[6] In fact, some psychoactive materials can interfere with the concentration shamanic work demands.

One of the interesting things about shamanism is that, when a drug is used, it is taken by the curer or healer rather than the patient, although there are exceptions when both partake. This contrast with modern Western medicine is easily understood if one considers that the shaman must do his healing work in an altered state of consciousness. The idea is to provide access to the hidden reality. Such work is the responsibility of the shaman, not the patient.

In its essence, shamanic initiation is experiential and often gradual, consisting of learning successfully how to achieve the shamanic state of consciousness, and to see and journey in that state; acquiring personal certainty and knowledge of one's own guardian spirit, and enlisting its assistance while in the shamanic state of consciousness; and learning successfully to help others as a shaman. A characteristic phase of more advanced shamanism is having personal certainty and knowledge of one's own spirit helpers. There are even more advanced phases, as well as some important kinds of shamanic experiences, that are not dealt with in this book. If you succeed in experiencing the first three phases listed above, however, you can probably call yourself a shaman. But shamanic initiation is a never-ending process of struggle and joy, and the definitive decisions about your status as a shaman will be made by those you try to help.

A new shaman, after learning the basic principles, methods, and cosmology of shamanism, builds personal knowledge and power by shamanic practice and journeying. As this knowledge is acquired, the shaman becomes a guide for other people. For example, a person in his community may have a dream or vision and ask the shaman about its meaning. The master shaman is able to say, "Oh yes, what you experienced fits in there . . ." on the basis of what he has experientially learned so far. The shaman is forever trying to articulate his personal revelatory experiences as though they were pieces of a great cosmic jigsaw puzzle. Many years of shamanic experience are usually necessary to arrive at a high degree of knowledge of the cosmic puzzle, and even a master shaman does not expect ever to complete the puzzle in a mortal lifetime.

A true master shaman does not challenge the validity of anybody else's experiences, although less capable and less humble shamans may. The master shaman will try to integrate even the most unusual experiences into his total cosmology, a cosmology based primarily on his own journeys. If he can do it easily he is probably a master, like the Conibo Indian shaman who told me, "Oh, they're always saying that."

The master shaman never says that what you experienced is a fantasy. That is one of the differences between shamanism and science. Yet there *are* similarities between the shaman and the scientist. The best of both are in awe of the complexity and magnificence of the universe and of Nature, and realize that during their own lifetimes they will only come to observe and understand a small portion of what is going on. Both shamans and scientists personally pursue research into the mysteries of the universe, and both believe that the underlying causal processes of that universe are hidden from ordinary view. And neither master shamans nor master scientists allow the dogma of ecclesiastical and political authorities to interfere with their explorations. It was no accident that Galileo was accused of witchcraft (shamanism).

The shaman is an empiricist. One of the definitions of empiricism is "the practice of emphasizing experience esp. of the senses" (Webster's Third New International Dictionary). And indeed the shaman depends primarily on firsthand experience, of the senses, to acquire knowledge. Still, the master shaman is humble. After all, none of us really knows what is going on. Everyone is limited to his own small window onto the universe. As a Mohave woman named Hama: Utce: said:

> Every shaman tells a different story of the creation. One may hear it told in several ways. All stories relate to the same event, but the way of telling it is different, as though different witnesses related it, remembering or forgetting different details. It is as though an Indian, a Negro and a Frenchman would tell it, or as though I, my husband, Hivsu: Tupo: ma (burnt raw) or you were describing a car accident we witnessed.[7]

Shamans are people of action as well as knowledge. They serve the community by moving into and out of the hidden reality when asked for help. But only a few shamans become true masters of knowledge, power, and healing. There is typically a great deal of critical evaluation by the people in their communities as to how proficient particular shamans are, how successful they are in healing people. Shamans' "track records" are well known, and people decide which shamans to go to in matters of life and death. So, although many people can become shamans, only a few are recognized as outstanding.

The Shamanic State of Consciousness

The shaman operates in nonordinary reality only a small portion of his time, and then only as needed to perform shamanic tasks, for shamanism is a part-time activity. Among the Jívaro, the Conibo, the Eskimo, and most other primitive groups, the master shaman is usually an active participant in the economic, social, and even political affairs of the community. He is commonly an accomplished hunter or gardener, craftsperson and artist, thinker, and responsible family and community member. Indeed, the ability of the master shaman to operate successfully in two different realities is seen as evidence of power.

He follows the precepts of shamanism when engaged in that kind of activity, and follows the precepts of ordinary reality when not engaged in shamanic work. The shaman moves back and forth between the two realities deliberately and with serious intention. Whichever the reality, the shaman thinks and acts in the ways appropriate to it, and has as his

46

objective the mastery of both his nonordinary activities and his ordinary activities. Only he who successfully masters his actions in both realms is a master shaman.

Both personal realities of the shaman, the nonordinary and the ordinary, have their correlative states of consciousness. Each reality may be coped with successfully only when one is in the state of consciousness appropriate to it. Thus, if one is crossing a busy city street, the proper state of consciousness is different from that to be employed in entering the shamanic Lowerworld. A master shaman is fully aware of the appropriate consciousness for each situation with which he is faced, and enters into that state of consciousness as needed.

A perception of two realities is typical of shamanism, even though some Western armchair philosophers have long denied the legitimacy of claiming such a dual division between the ordinary world and a hidden world among primitive peoples, apparently assuming that primitives cannot distinguish between the two. As I earlier explained, the Jívaro not only make such a division consciously, but they ascribe much greater importance to the nonordinary or hidden one.[8] I agree with Åke Hultkrantz when he says:

> . . . If such [primitive] peoples do not consciously make such a dichotomy—which they sometimes do—they do in fact unconsciously order their cognitions according to this model. One proof of this is the shamanistic trance. The world of ecstasy is the world of supernatural powers and agencies, therefore the shaman dives into it. He exists in two worlds: outside the trance he lives the daily life of his tribesmen, inside the trance he is part and parcel of the supernatural world, sharing with the spirits some of their potentialities: the capacity to fly, to transform himself, to become one with his helping spirit, and so on.[9]

The emphasis I make here on drawing a distinction between the experiences one has in the SSC and the OSC, or that Castaneda makes between nonordinary reality and ordinary reality, is not a distinction that is usually noted in the conversations of shamans among themselves or even with Westerners. Thus, if you were to listen to a Jívaro shaman talk, you might hear in his everyday conversation accounts of experiences and deeds which could seem to you, as a Westerner, to be patently absurd or impossible. For example, he might tell you of splitting a large tree at a distance with his shamanic power, or that he saw an inverted rainbow inside the chest of a neighbor. In the same breath, he might tell you that he is making a new blowgun, or that he went hunting the previous morning.

The problem is not, as some Western philosophers would have it, that primitive peoples such as the Jívaro exhibit a primitive "prelogical" mind. The problem is that the Westerner is simply unsophisticated from a shamanic point of view. For his fellow tribespeople, the Jívaro does not need to specify which state of consciousness he was in to have a particular experience. They immediately know, because they have already learned what kinds of experiences occur in the SSC and what kind occur in the OSC. Only the Western outsider lacks this background.

The Jívaro sophistication is far from unique; in fact, it is probably true throughout virtually all of the shamanic cultures. Unfortunately, Western observers, lacking extensive experience with altered states of consciousness, altogether too often failed to inquire as to the cognitive state in which their native informants were when they had "impossible" experiences. As the Australian anthropologist W. E. H. Stanner properly observes:

> It is fatally easy for Europeans, encountering such things for the first time, to go on to suppose that "mysticism" of this kind rules *all* aboriginal thought. It is not so. "Logical" thought and "rational" conduct are about as widely present in aboriginal life as they are on the simpler levels of European life. . . . And if one wishes to see a really brilliant demonstration of deductive thought, one has only to see [an aborigine] tracking a wounded kangaroo, and persuade him to say why he interprets given signs in a certain way.[10]

In other words, the limitations are not those of primitive peoples, but our own in understanding the two-tiered nature of their experiences and the respect they accord them. Because our Western culture is not shamanic, it is necessary in teaching shamanism to make clear the distinctions between the SSC and the OSC, or between nonordinary reality and ordinary reality, as Castaneda does. When and if you become a shaman, and if there are other shamans with whom you can converse, you will find it no more necessary than a Jívaro or an Australian aborigine to specify the state of consciousness you were in when you had a particular experience. Your audience, if composed of persons of knowledge, will know.

The altered state of consciousness component of the SSC includes varying degrees of trance, ranging from essentially light (as with many North American Indian shamans), to very deep (as among the Lapps, where a shaman may temporarily appear comatose). Indeed, this entire range is reported for Siberian shamans. As Hultkrantz points out, "Pronouncements to the effect that the shamanic trance is invariably of the same depth are therefore misleading."[11] Similarly, Eliade observes: "Among the Ugrians shamanic ecstasy is less a trance than a 'state of inspiration'; the shaman sees and hears spirits; he is 'carried out of himself' because he is journeying in ecstasy through distant regions, but he is not unconscious. He is a visionary and inspired. However, the basic experience is ecstatic, and the principal means of obtaining it is, as in other regions, magico-religious music."[12]

What *is* definite is that *some* degree of alteration of consciousness is necessary to shamanic practice. Outside Western observers have frequently failed to be aware that a shaman was in a light trance, precisely because they were external observers lacking personal shamanic experience. Hultkrantz quite properly notes:

> A shaman may seem to act in a lucid state when, in actual fact, his mind is occupied with interior visions. I have myself witnessed a North American medicine-man operate during curing in a twilight context not easily discovered by an outsider; and his testimony to me afterwards of what he saw during his curing stressed the fact that he had been in a light trance.[13]

At an earlier, critical point in his life, before taking up shamanism, the shaman may have entered this altered state of consciousness very deeply, although there are many individual and cultural exceptions. Sometimes such an experience occurs in an intentional vision quest to get guardian spirit power. Other times it occurs at the climax of a serious illness, as among some North and South American Indians, as well as in native Siberia. Such a radically profound and revelatory experience often encourages the individual to take up the way of the shaman. My own first psychedelic experience among the Conibo Indians in 1961 is a personal example.

The word "trance" will be generally avoided here, because our Western cultural conceptions with regard to this term often carry the implication that it is a nonconscious state. Reinhard similarly avoids the use of "trance," noting, ". . . what we are really trying to establish is that the shaman is in a nonordinary psychic state which in some cases means not a loss of consciousness but rather an altered state of consciousness."[14] *

It is in the SSC that one "sees" shamanically. This may be called "visualizing," "imaging," or, as expressed by Australian aborigines, using "the strong eye."[15] Although such *seeing* is done in an altered state of consciousness, it would be an unempirical prejudgment inimical to achieving firsthand understanding to dismiss such visions as hallucinations. As the distinguished Australian anthropologist A. P. Elkin observes, the vision of an aborigine shaman "is no mere hallucination. It is a mental formation visualized and externalized, which may even exist for a time independent of its creator. . . . While the person is experiencing the vision, he cannot move, but he is conscious of what is going on around him. As one [shaman] of the Kattang tribe, N. S. W. [Australia], told me . . . he could see and know what was happening, but was as one dead, feeling nothing."[16]

The SSC normally permits full recall later of the experience when the shaman has returned to the OSC, unlike the characteristic trance of the Western spirit medium or of the participant in Caribbean or Javanese spirit possession dances.[17] In other words, the SSC does not typically involve amnesia. In the SSC, part of the shaman's consciousness is usually still lightly connected to the ordinary reality of the physical or material environment where he is located. The lightness of his trance is a reason that a drumbeat often must be maintained by an assistant to sustain him in the SSC. If the drumming stops, he might come back rapidly to the OSC, and thus fail in his work.

Basic tools for entering the SSC are the drum and rattle. The shaman generally restricts use of his drum and rattle to evoking and maintaining the SSC, and thus his unconscious mind comes automatically to associate their use with serious shamanic work. The beginning of the steady, monotonous sound of the rattle and the drum, which has been repeatedly associated with the SSC on previous

* Probably the most commonly accepted definition of an altered state of consciousness is by Arnold M. Ludwig, who describes it as "any mental state(s) induced by various physiological, psychological, or pharmacological maneuvers or agents, which can be recognized subjectively by the individual himself (or by an objective observer of the individual) as representing a sufficient deviation in subjective experience or psychological functioning from certain general norms for that individual during alert, waking consciousness." (Ludwig 1972:11.) A problem with Ludwig's definition is that it may carry the implication that an "alert, waking" state may not characterize an altered state of consciousness. While the shaman is occasionally sometimes neither alert nor waking in the SSC, commonly he is very alert even if not in a fully waking state; and very commonly in the SSC he is both alert and waking. Katz (1976a: 282-283), in his study of !Kung Bushmen trance-healing, also expresses some reservations about Ludwig's definition.

occasions, becomes a signal to his brain to return to the SSC. For an experienced shaman, accordingly, just a few minutes of the familiar rattling and/or drumming is usually sufficient to achieve the light trance in which most shamanic work is done.

The repetitive sound of the drum is usually fundamental to undertaking shamanic tasks in the SSC. With good reason, Siberian and other shamans sometimes refer to their drums as the "horse" or "canoe" that transports them into the Lowerworld or Upperworld. The steady, monotonous beat of the drum acts like a carrier wave, first to help the shaman enter the SSC, and then to sustain him on his journey.

The importance of the drum as a "mount" or "steed" is illustrated by these shamanic verses from the Soyot (Tuvas) of Siberia:

Shaman Drums

Oh! My many-colored drum
Ye who standeth in the forward corner!
Oh! My merry and painted drum,
Ye who standeth here!
Let thy shoulder and neck be strong.

Hark, oh hark my horse—ye female maral deer!
Hark, oh hark my horse—ye bear!
Hark, oh hark ye [bear]!

Oh, painted drum who standeth in the forward corner!
My mounts—male and female maral deer.
Be silent sonorous drum,
Skin-covered drum,
Fulfill my wishes

Like flitting clouds, carry me
Through the lands of dusk
And below the leaden sky,
Sweep along like wind
Over the mountain peaks! [18]

Laboratory research by Neher has demonstrated that drumming produces changes in the central nervous system. The rhythmic stimulation affects the electrical activity in "many sensory and motor areas of the brain, not ordinarily affected, through their connections with the sensory area being stimulated." [19] This appears to be due in part to the fact that the single beat of a drum contains many sound

51

frequencies, and accordingly it simultaneously transmits impulses along a variety of nerve pathways in the brain. Furthermore, drum beats are mainly of low frequency, which means that more energy can be transmitted to the brain by a drum beat than from a sound stimulus of higher frequency. This is possible, Neher states, because "the low frequency receptors of the ear are more resistant to damage than the delicate high frequency receptors and can withstand higher amplitudes of sound before pain is felt."[20]

Recent research on the shamanistic spirit dances of the Salish Indians of the Northwest Coast supports and expands Neher's findings on the capacity of rhythmic drumming to induce an altered state of consciousness. Jilek and Ormestad found that drum beat frequencies in the theta wave EEG frequency range (four to seven cycles per second) predominated during initiation procedures using the Salish deer-skin drum. This is the frequency range, Jilek notes, that "is expected to be most effective in the production of trance states."[21]

It is hoped that such research will eventually be accompanied by the telemetering of the EEG of shamans while they are engaged in SSC work. It seems likely that this kind of investigation will lead to the finding that the SSC commonly involves the theta level as well as the less-deep alpha level.

The shaking of the shaman's rattle provides stimulation to higher frequency pathways in the brain than does the drum, reinforcing the drum beats and further heightening the total sonic effect. While of a higher frequency, the sound of most rattles is of a sufficiently low amplitude as not to cause pain in the ear receptors.

While the shaman may beat the drum himself when entering the SSC, his full arrival there requires an assistant to take over the task of maintaining the drumming, as among the Tungus of Siberia, so that the shaman's altered state of consciousness will be maintained.[22] An alternate technique among the Tungus is to let all the drumming be done by an assistant, even before the shaman enters the SSC. This is the method I prefer, since otherwise the physical demands of beating a drum can interfere with my transition into the SSC. The shaman should, however, still regulate the speed of the drumming, for only he can sense the appropriateness of the tempo. In the techniques I have adopted, I shake a rattle, typically starting at a slow tempo and increasing it as I feel the need. The sound of the rattle not only provides the lead for the drummer, but also supplements the sonic drive of the drum with a higher frequency input. When the shaman using this method finally enters the SSC, he is no longer able to shake the rattle, so the drummer carries on for him, continuing the drumming in the tempo last heard from the rattle.

When the Tungus shaman's assistant does all the drumming, however, the shaman does not use a rattle. Instead, he sets the tempo by dancing, the rhythm of the bells and iron trinkets on his costume leading the drum and supplementing it with higher frequency sounds.[23] This is a technique which provides a body motion input into the shaman's nervous system that matches the sounds since, as Shirokogoroff observes, ". . . the 'dancing' is partly called forth by the necessity of producing rhythmic sounds."[24]

The change into an SSC is also helped by singing. The shaman typically has special "power songs" that he chants on such occasions. While the words may vary somewhat from shaman to shaman in a particular tribe, usually the melody and rhythm of the songs are not the invention of the individual shaman but are shared in a particular tribal region.

The songs tend to be repetitive and relatively monotonous, mainly increasing in tempo as the shaman approaches the SSC. They may have the latent function of affecting central nervous system activity in a manner analogous to yogic breathing exercises, although I know of no research carried out to determine this. The shaman is often helped into the SSC by the members of the audience, who join him in the singing. The words help evoke the SSC, tending to refer to the shaman's spiritual guardians and helpers, and to reaffirm his power.

The learned component of the SSC includes the ascription of full reality to the things one sees, feels, hears, and otherwise experiences in the altered state of consciousness. These firsthand, empirical experiences are not viewed by the shaman as fantasy, but as immediate reality. At the same time, the shaman recognizes the separateness of the SSC reality from that of the OSC, and does not confuse the two. He knows when he is in one or the other, and enters each by choice.

The learned precepts used while he is in the SSC include the assumption that animals, plants, humans, and other phenomena seen in an altered state of consciousness are fully real, within the context of the nonmaterial, or nonordinary, reality in which they are perceived. The shaman enters the SSC to see and interact with these nonmaterial forms. Such forms are not visible to the shaman or others when in the OSC, and do not constitute part of ordinary reality.

The learned aspect of the SSC involves a deep respect for all forms of life, with a humble awareness of our dependence on the plants, animals, and even inorganic matter of our planet. The shaman knows that humans are related to all forms of life, that they are "all our relations," as the Lakota Sioux say. In both the SSC and the OSC the shaman approaches the other forms of life with familial respect and understanding. He recognizes their antiquity, relatedness, and special strengths.

The shaman accordingly enters the SSC with a reverence for Nature, for the inherent strengths of the wild animal and plant species, and for their tenacious abilities to survive and flourish through eons of planetary existence. Approached in an altered state of consciousness with respect and love, Nature, he believes, is prepared to reveal things not ascertainable in an ordinary state of consciousness.

Many North American Indian tribes still preserve an essentially shamanic view of reality as, for example, in this statement by a Hopi:

> To the Hopi all life is one—it is the same. This world where he lives is the human world and in it all the animals, birds, insects, and every living creature, as well as the trees and plants which also have life, appear only in masquerade, or in the forms in which we ordinarily see them. But it is said that all these creatures and these living things that share the spark of life with us humans, surely have other homes where they live in human forms like ourselves. Therefore, all these living things are thought of as human and they may sometimes be seen in their own forms even on earth. If they are killed, then the soul of this creature may return to its own world which it may never leave again, but the descendants of this creature will take its place in the human world, generation after generation.[25]

Even in broad daylight, one can learn to see shamanically the nonordinary aspects of natural phenomena. For example, the following is a method of *rock-seeing,* a technique I learned from a Lakota Sioux medicine man. First decide upon a problem for which you wish an answer. Then simply walk through a wild area until a two-fisted-size stone on the ground seems to attract your attention. Pick it up and carry it to a spot where you can comfortably sit down with it.

Place the stone on the ground in front of you, and pose the question to which you want an answer. Carefully study the upper surface of the stone until you are able to see one or more living creatures formed by its lines, crevices and other irregularities. It may take a few minutes. When you are satisfied that you have discerned one or more animals, plants, insects, faces, human forms, or other entities on the stone's surface, then think about what the stone is trying to tell you about the problem you have posed. Fix your conclusion in your mind and then turn the rock over. Repeat the same process of seeing and thinking using the new surface. If the stone is thick enough, you can repeat the process again with the remaining two sides of the stone.

Next, quietly contemplate how the individual communications from each of the four sides can be put together to form a message that constitutes an answer to your question. Then respectfully, and with thanks, return the stone to the position and place where you found it.

Once you have gained enough shamanic experience, you can use this technique to help another person. Have the person go through the same steps as above. The difference is that you both participate in seeing the answer to his problem. As each side is viewed, let him first describe and analyze what he sees. Then you, as the shaman, supplement his observations and analysis with your own. On the basis of your greater experience, you may be able to suggest how what you see fits in with what he sees. Then turn the stone over and repeat the process for all four sides. Finally, the person makes his own synthesis of the four sides into a general answer to his problem.

Obviously, there are similarities and differences between this shamanic approach and a Rorschach test or psychoanalytic techniques of free association. But the fact that there are differences does not make the shamanic technique operationally inferior. From the shaman's perspective, there *are* animals and beings in the stone. The concept of fantasy has no place in the shaman's world. For him, all of nature has a hidden, nonordinary reality. That is something one learns to see in following the shaman's way.

This free adaptation by David Cloutier of a shaman's poem from the Chukchee tribe of Siberia illustrates what I am talking about:

Things a Shaman Sees

Everything that is
is alive

on a steep river bank
there's a voice that speaks
I've seen the master of that voice
he bowed to me
I spoke with him
he answers all my questions

55

everything that is
is alive

Little gray bird
little blue breast
sings in a hollow bough
she calls her spirits dances
sings her shaman songs
woodpecker on a tree
that's his drum
he's got a drumming nose
and the tree shakes
cries out like a drum
when the axe bites its side

all these things answer
my call

everything that is
is alive

the lantern walks around
the walls of this house have tongues
even this bowl has its own true home
the hides asleep in their bags
were up talking all night
antlers on the graves
rise and circle the mounds
while the dead themselves get up
and go visit the living ones[26]

CHAPTER 4

Power Animals

Shamans have long believed their powers were the powers of the animals, of the plants, of the sun, of the basic energies of the universe. In the garden Earth they have drawn upon their assumed powers to help save other humans from illness and death, to provide strength in daily life, to commune with their fellow creatures, and to live a joyful existence in harmony with the totality of Nature.

Millennia before Charles Darwin, people in shamanic cultures were convinced that humans and animals were related. In their myths, for example, the animal characters were commonly portrayed as essentially human in physical form but individually distinguished by the particular personality characteristics possessed by the various types of animals as they exist in the wild today. Thus Coyote is distinguished in the stories by his mischievous behavior, and Raven often by his unseemly dependence on others to kill game for him. Then, according to various creation myths, the animals became physically differentiated into the forms in which they are found today. Accordingly, the myths explain, it is no longer possible for humans and animals to converse together, or for animals to have human form.

While the mythical paradise of animal-human unity is lost in ordinary reality, it still remains accessible in nonordinary reality to the shaman and vision-seeker. The Australian aborigines' concept of "The Dream Time" embodies this awareness, for it refers to a mythological past that still exists parallel in time to present-day ordinary reality, and which is penetrated in dreams and visions.[1] The shaman, alone of the humans, is regularly able to effect the animal-human unity by entering the SSC. For the shaman in the altered state of consciousness, the mythical past is immediately accessible.

North and South American Indian mythology is pervaded with animal characters in tales that tell not of the adventures of *a* coyote, *a* raven, or *a* bear, but of the adventures of Coyote, Raven, and Bear. In other words, the individual characters represent entire species or larger classes of animals. This is analogous to the unity of one's individual guardian animal spirit with the entire genus or species to which it belongs. This unity means that a person usually possesses not just the power of a bear, or of an eagle, but the power of Bear or of Eagle. The possessor of a guardian animal normally draws upon the spiritual power of its entire genus or species, although he is indeed connected into that power by an individualized manifestation of it.

The connectedness between humans and the animal world is very basic in shamanism, with the shaman utilizing his knowledge and methods to participate in the power of that world. Through his guardian spirit or power animal, the shaman connects with the power of the animal world, the mammals, birds, fish, and other beings. The shaman has to have a particular guardian in order to do his work, and his guardian helps him in certain special ways.

The guardian spirit is sometimes referred to by native North Americans as the *power animal,* as among the Coast Salish and the Okanagon of Washington.[2] This is a particularly apt term, for it emphasizes the power-giving aspect of the guardian spirit as well as the frequency with which it is perceived as an animal. But the Coast Salish also sometimes refer to the guardian spirit as the *Indian,* for it can appear to them in human form as well.[3] Such an animal-human duality of the guardian spirit is a common feature of North and South American Indian cosmology as well as elsewhere in the primitive world. Thus, among the Cocopa of the Colorado River valley, animals appear in dreams as human beings.[4] Among the Jívaro, a guardian spirit usually first appears in a vision as an animal, and then in a dream as a human.[5]

The ability of animals to appear as humans is not surprising, given the widespread belief that humans and animals are biologically related (are "relations") and in ancient times were able to converse together. In nonordinary reality, the animals continue to be able to manifest themselves in human forms to humans who have entered the SSC. It is only the shaman, or the person with shamanistic tendencies, who is able to resume the lost ability to communicate with the (other) animals. Thus, when a man becomes a shaman among the tribes of the western desert of South Australia, he acquires the power to speak to birds and other animals.[6] When Castaneda engages in conversation with a coyote, he is making progress toward becoming a shaman.[7] Among the Jívaro, in fact, if an animal speaks to you, it is considered evidence that the animal is your guardian spirit.

Among the Lakota Sioux, the guardian animal spirits often speak when they appear to the vision seeker. As Lame Deer recounts, "All of a sudden I heard a big bird crying, and then quickly he hit me on the back, touched me with his spread wings. I heard the cry of an eagle, loud above the voices of many other birds. It seemed to say, 'We have been waiting for you. We knew you would come. Now you are here. Your trail leads from here . . . you will have a ghost with you always— another self.' "[8]

The capability of the guardian animal spirits to speak to a human or to manifest themselves sometimes in human forms is taken as an indication of their power. Another indication of their power is when they make themselves visible navigating in an element that is not their "ordinary" environment. Common examples are a land mammal or serpent flying through the air, with or without the benefit of wings. All these capabilities show that the animal is indeed nonordinary, a bearer of power, able to transcend the nature of an ordinary animal and its ordinary existence. When its transformation into human form occurs, it is a magical act of power. When possessed by a shaman, the power animal acts as an alter ego, imparting to the shaman the power of transformation, and especially the power of transformation *from* human to the power animal, as well as back again.

The belief by shamans that they can metamorphose into the form of their guardian animal spirit or power animal is widespread and obviously ancient. Among the Arunta of Australia they often took on the form of eagle-hawks.[9] In the course of the initiation of a shaman of the Wiradjeri tribe in Australia, he had the nonordinary experience that feathers emerged from his arms and grew into wings. Then he was taught to fly. Subsequently he "sang off his wings," and returning to ordinary reality, walked back into camp and discussed his experience.[10]

59

In northernmost Scandinavia, Lapp shamans changed into wolves, bears, reindeer, and fish; and Siberian and Eskimo shamans frequently transformed themselves into wolves.[11] Similarly, among the Yuki Indians of California, shamans who were believed to have the power to transform themselves into bears were called "bear doctors." The bear doctor of the Yuki "was really a shaman who had the bear as a guardian spirit."[12] An incipient bear shaman "associated with actual bears, and ate their food, and at times lived with them," sometimes for an entire summer.[13]

The ancient shamanic belief in the ability to transform oneself into an animal survived in Western Europe until the Renaissance.[14] The Christian Church, of course, considered persons engaged in animal metamorphosis to be wizards, witches, and sorcerers, and persecuted them through the Inquisition. Yet a colleague of Galileo, the alchemist and scientist Giovanni Battista Porta, in 1562 still possessed the ancient knowledge of how to experience such a metamorphosis and published the information in his famous book, *Natural Magick*.[15] Thus he explains how, using a hallucinogenic potion, a man would "believe he was changed into a Bird or Beast." Porta observed, "the man would seem sometimes to be changed into a fish; and flinging out his arms, would swim on the Ground: sometimes he would seem to skip up, and then to dive down again. Another would believe himself turned into a Goose, and would eat Grass, and beat the Ground with his Teeth, like a Goose: now and then sing, and endeavor to clap his Wings."[16] Similarly, Castaneda, with the aid of a hallucinogenic mixture, reports he had the experience of becoming a crow, and that don Genaro observed that shamans can become eagles and owls.[17]

The use of a hallucinogenic drug, however, is by no means necessary for a person to experience the metamorphosis into a bird or other animal. Dancing, accompanied by drumming, is the far more common method employed by shamans throughout much of the primitive world to achieve a shamanic state of consciousness sufficient to having the experience. The initiation of shamans among the Carib Indians of northern South America, for example, involves nighttime dancing during which the neophytes move in imitation of animals. This is part of a process of learning how to turn into animals.[18]

But it is not just shamans and shamanic initiates who utilize dancing to metamorphose into animal forms. In many primitive cultures, anyone with a guardian spirit may use dancing as a means of evoking his alter ego. Among the Coast Salish Indians of the Northwest Coast, the winter dance season provides an opportunity for an individual to consciously become one with his power animal.[19] "The dancer's spirit finds its dramatized expression in dance steps, tempo, movements, miens and gestures: in the sneaking pace, then flying leaps of the ferociously yelling 'warrior,' or in the swaying trot of the plump, sadly weeping 'bear mother'; in the rubber-like reptilian writhing of the 'double headed serpent' . . . in the 'lizard' who sheds tears over his devoured offspring or in the mighty 'whale' who grabs smaller fish."[20] Often Northwest Coast shamans doing such dancing wore special masks and accoutrements to add to the unification with their power animals. Among the Tsimshian, for example, a shaman might dance not only wearing the mask of an eagle, but also claws of copper.[21] The desire for unity with animals of power is well illustrated by this version by Cloutier of a grizzly bear song from the Tlingit tribe of the Northwest Coast:

Whu! Bear!
Whu
Whu

So you say
Whu Whu Whu!
You come

You're a fine young man
You Grizzly Bear
You crawl out of your fur

You come
I say Whu Whu Whu!
I throw grease in the fire

For you
Grizzly Bear
We're one![22]

Much animal-like dancing in the primitive world has as its objective the unification of power animals with the dancers, whether or not the rituals are purely shamanic in other respects. Thus the dance of the Beast Gods by the shamanistic medicine societies at Zuni Pueblo in the American Southwest bears "a strong resemblance to séances among other peoples in which the shaman is inspired, in that the Beast Gods are summoned by dancing, rattling, and drumming, and the dancers work themselves into a frenzied condition in which they imitate the actions and cries of animals."[23] Those dancers assuming the personality of the bear may even wear actual bear paws over their hands.[24] But this dance of the Beast Gods is more than simple imitation, since the Zuni dancer, like a North American Plains Indian doing an Eagle or Buffalo Dance, is striving to go beyond imitation to become one with the animal. Thus, the Osage Indian song series, "The Rising of the Buffalo Bull Men," emphasizes the creation of a personal consciousness of unity with the animal:

I rise, I rise,
I, whose tread makes the earth to rumble.

I rise, I rise,
I, in whose thighs there is strength.

I rise, I rise,
I, who whips his back with his tail when in rage.

I rise, I rise,
I, in whose humped shoulder there is power.

I rise, I rise,
I, who shakes his mane when angered.

I rise, I rise,
I, whose horns are sharp and curved.[25]

Likewise, a Zuni dancer wearing the mask of one of the *kachina* gods is doing more than impersonating the *kachina*. Transported into an altered state of consciousness by the dancing, drumming, rattling, and whirr of bull roarers, he "becomes for the time being the actual embodiment of the spirit which is believed to reside in the mask."[26] As one Coast Salish said, "When I dance I don't act, just follow your power, just follow the way of your power."[27]

Shamans, in dancing their guardian animal spirits, commonly not only make the movements of the power animals but also the sounds. In Siberia, native North and South America, and elsewhere, shamans make bird calls and the cries, growls, and other sounds of their animal powers when experiencing their transformations.[28] As Lame Deer says of bear power, "We make bear sounds . . . 'Harrnh' . . ."[29] Similarly, Castaneda growls and makes a gesture of claws in response to don Juan's advice that showing his claws is "good practice."[30]

What Lame Deer is speaking of is not the uncontrollable possession of the Carribean Vodun cults, but rather a reaffirmation by the shaman of his oneness with his animal companion. As Eliade notes, this is "less a possession than a magical transformation of the shaman into that animal."[31]

Among the Indians of Mexico and Guatemala, the guardian spirit is commonly known by the term, "nagual," derived from the Aztec *nahualli*. "Nagual" refers to both a guardian animal spirit and to the shaman who changes into that power animal (compound words derived from *nahualli* have the meaning of being "disguised, masked").[32] "Nagual" is also commonly applied in Mexico to a shaman who is *capable* of making such a transformation, whether he is doing it at the time or not. Thus Castaneda refers to don Juan as a nagual, in addition to speaking of the broader ramifications of the concept.[33]

Incidentally, Castaneda contrasts the nagual with the "tonal" in a lengthy, if somewhat confusing discussion.[34] The confusion can be somewhat dissipated if one understands that "tonal" derives from the Nahuatl or Aztec term, *tonalli*. This word referred especially to one's vital soul, and the sign of one's day of birth, which was frequently an animal. The *tonalli* was part of an elaborate calendrical system with implications of predestination, somewhat analogous to one's sign in Western astrology. Thus the tonal concept carries the implications of fate, predestination, and the destiny of one's life from birth to death. Castaneda's discussion is generally consistent with this understanding.[35] Thus one's life experiences in ordinary reality may be believed to be determined by the tonal animal; but this animal is not the same as the nagual of the shaman, which like guardian animal spirits elsewhere is connected with the SSC and, as Castaneda implies, lies beyond ordinary reality.

A confusion between a tonal animal and the nagual animal sometimes occurs in the anthropological literature on Mexico and Guatemala. This may be due both to faulty scholarship and to the merging of the two animals in their cosmologies by some native Mexican and Guatemalan groups in colonial times.[36]

While for some tribes it is reported that virtually every adult had a guardian spirit, as among the Nitlakapamuk Indians of British Columbia or the Twana of western Washington, the more usual situation was that not all adults possessed guardian spirits.[37] Thus, among the North American Plains Indians, individuals frequently failed to obtain them, and as a result were usually considered to be doomed to lack power and success in life. Among the Jívaro, most adult males believed themselves to possess them, having the certain knowledge that they had succeeded in the vision quest at the sacred waterfall. It was not so essential for women to obtain them formally, because the intra-tribal feuds, the most common cause of violent death, were primarily directed at adult males rather than at women and children.[38]

The most famous method of acquiring a guardian spirit is the vision quest or vigil conducted in a solitary wilderness location, as among the Plains tribes of North America.[39] The Jívaro pilgrimage to a sacred waterfall is a South American example of such a vision quest. Even among the Jívaro, however, the beneficial power of a guardian spirit could be acquired without going on a vision quest. Parents of a newly born infant, in fact, typically gave it a mild hallucinogen so that it could "see" and hopefully thus acquire an *arutam wakanI* or guardian spirit. The parents, of course, wanted the baby to have as much protection as possible in order to survive into adult life. There was also a somewhat stronger hallucinogen, *uchich maikua,* or "children's datura," that was administered for the same purpose when the child was somewhat older, but not yet ready to undertake the vision quest at the sacred waterfall.

The Jívaro assumed that a child would probably not even reach the age of six, seven, or eight without some protection from a guardian spirit. The parents, however, could never be sure that an infant or very small child had really obtained a vision and power, so it was considered essential for a boy eventually to go on the formal vision quest to be absolutely sure he had the protection of a guardian spirit. Life was perceived as not as dangerous for females as for males in that feud-ridden society, but girls did have a smaller version of the vision quest in the forest near the house.

In North America, the Southern Okanagon of the State of Washington held a view similar to that of the Jívaro. Among the Okanagon, guardian spirits commonly were acquired involuntarily by very young children without going on a vision quest.[40] Small children's visions were usually similar to those seen on the formal vision quest by youths and young adults. "The spirit first appeared as human, but as it departed the child saw what kind of animal it was. It might come without any forethought on the part of child or parent, and at any time of day or night."[41] Walter Cline reports:

Only a very precocious child would know about his guardian spirit at the age of four or five. . . . Unless he were "very smart" [even a youth or

64

young adult] immediately forgot the vision and what the spirit had said to him, and, in most cases, had no intercourse with the spirit for a number of years . . . In the event of serious emergency during this time, however, it was ready to help him.[42]

In other words, it is possible for a person to have, or to have had, the past protection and power of a guardian spirit without being conscious of it. Thus, in 1957, a Jívaro shaman *saw* that I had a guardian spirit even though I myself was unaware of it.

To a shaman it is readily apparent that many Westerners have guardian spirits, as evidenced by their energy, good health, and other outward manifestations of their power. It is tragic, from the point of view of such a shaman, that even these power-full people are nonetheless ignorant of the source of their power and thus do not know how to utilize it fully. A related tragedy, from the same point of view, is that lethargic, ill, and dispirited Western adults have obviously lost the guardian spirits that protected them through their childhood. Worse, they do not even know that there is a method to regain them.

Calling the Beasts

Now try an exercise in which you will have a chance to get in touch with one or more of your unknown past or present guardian spirits. You probably had at least one in the past, or otherwise you would not have survived childhood's hazards and illnesses. Even if it has long since left you, the exercise should awaken your hidden memories of it. This exercise is a simple, ancient shamanic technique. One name for it is "Calling the Beasts." There are different names for it in different cultures. It is a way whereby the people of the community, through dance, evoke or get in touch with their animal aspects.

Keep in mind that a single guardian spirit can appear either in animal or human form, although most likely you will see or feel the *animal* aspect of your guardian spirit.

Undertake this exercise in a quiet, half-darkened room free of any furniture that might interfere with your movements. It will help if you have two good rattles (see Appendix A on drums and rattles). Do not hesitate, however, to try this exercise without waiting to acquire rattles. There are two phases in the exercise: (1) the starting dance, and (2) dancing your animal. In both dances you steadily and loudly shake a rattle in each hand, and your dancing is in time with the rattles. In all the dancing you keep your eyes half-closed. This allows you to cut down

65

on light, and at the same time enables you to know where you are in the room.

The Starting Dance

1. Standing still and erect, face east and shake one rattle very rapidly and strongly four times. This is the signal that you are starting, ending, or making an important transition in serious shamanic work. Think of the rising sun, that ultimately brings power to all living things. (A total time of about 20 seconds.)

2. Still facing east, start shaking one rattle at a steady rate of about 150 times per minute, standing in place. Do this about half a minute to each of the cardinal directions (rotating either clockwise or counterclockwise, depending on what seems better for you). Meanwhile, think of your plant and animal relatives in all the four directions who are ready to help you. Now face east again and shake the rattle above your head at the same rate for half a minute. Think of the sun, moon, stars, and the entire universe above. Next shake the rattle toward the ground in the same way. Think of the Earth, our home. (A total time of about 3 minutes.)

3. Still facing east, take both rattles in your hands and start shaking them at the same rate as in Step 2, simultaneously dancing as if you were jogging in place to the tempo of the rattles. In this starting dance, you are giving proof of your own sincerity to the power animals, wherever they may be, by making a self-sacrifice of your own energy to them in the form of dance. This dancing is a way of praying, and of evoking the sympathy of the guardian animal spirits. In shamanism it can truly be said that you dance to raise your spirits. (A total time of about 5 minutes.)

4. Stop dancing, and repeat Step 1. This signals you are about to make a significant transition to dancing your animal.

Dancing Your Animal

5. Start shaking your rattles loudly and slowly about 60 times per minute, moving your feet in the same tempo. Move slowly and in a free form around the room, trying to pick up the feeling of having some kind of mammal, bird, fish, reptile, or combination of these. Once you pick up the sense of some such animal, concentrate on it, and slowly move your body in accordance with being that animal. You are now touching the SSC. Be open to experiencing the emotions of that animal, and don't hesitate to make cries or noises of it, if you experience the desire. By keeping your eyes half-closed you may also see the nonordinary

environment in which the animal is moving, and perhaps even see the animal as well. Being and seeing the animal commonly happen simultaneously in the SSC. (The time for this tends to average about 5 minutes.)

6. Without pausing, shift into a faster rate of rattle-shaking and movement, about 100 shakes per minute. Continue everything else as in Step 5. (The time for this tends to average about 4 minutes.)

7. Without stopping, increase your rattle-shaking to approximately 180 times per minute, continuing your dancing as before, but at a still faster rate. (The time for this usually is about 4 minutes.)

8. Stop dancing, and mentally welcome the animal to stay in your body. As you do this, shake the rattles rapidly four times, drawing them toward your chest. (Time about 10 seconds.)

9. Repeat Step 1. This is the signal that the work is ended.

For a more powerful transition into the SSC when doing the above exercise, I recommend that a drum be used in addition to the rattles. For this, you will need someone to act as your assistant to beat the drum exactly in tempo with your shaking of the rattles (for information on drums, see Appendix A). Your assistant should stand at the side of the room and not attempt to participate in any of the movements while drumming. When the drummer becomes experienced with the steps of the exercise, you may find it possible to do the animal dancing without the rattles, thereby freeing your consciousness more from ordinary reality.

Typically, Westerners "dancing their animals" discover themselves to be such creatures as Crane, Tiger, Fox, Eagle, Bear, Deer, Porpoise, and even Dragon (for there are no "mythical" animals in the SSC; Dragon is as real as the others). One thing that usually becomes clear to the dancers is that underneath our ordinary human cultural consciousness is a near-universal emotional connection with wild animal alter egos.

Keep in mind that no matter how successful you were in dancing your animal, that in itself is not proof that you still have its power. You may only be dancing a memory. A successful experience does suggest, however, that you may have at least had such a guardian spirit in the past, if not now. The dancing itself, however, is no proof in itself, one way or another.

Incidentally, no matter how fierce a guardian animal spirit may seem, its possessor is in no danger because the power animal is absolutely harmless. It is only a source of power; it has no aggressive intentions. It only comes to you because you need help.

If one wishes to maintain shamanic practice, one has to change into one's animal regularly to keep the animal contented enough to stay. This involves exercising the animal through dance, singing songs of the animal, and recognizing "big" dreams as messages from the guardian, the power animal. Dancing your animal is an important method for keeping it content and thus making it reluctant to leave you. The guardian animal spirit resident in the mind-body of a person wants to have the enjoyment of once again existing in material form. It is a trade-off, for the person gets the power of the whole genus or species of animals represented by that guardian spirit. Just as a human may want to experience nonordinary reality by becoming a shaman, so too a guardian spirit may wish to experience ordinary reality by entering the body of a living human.

Even with the best of care, as I learned from the Jívaro years ago, guardian spirits usually stay with you only a few years and then depart. So, in the course of a long, powerful life, you will have a number of them one after another, whether you know it or not.

Dancing is not the only way you can physically exercise your power animal and keep it willing to stay with you. Another way is to exercise it in wilderness areas or, lacking that, remote areas of public parks. I remember one young Westerner trained in shamanism who worked weekdays in a bookstore and on Sundays went to a regional park where he took his Cougar for lopes over the hills. No one ever stopped him, and he found it more satisfying than going to church.

Of course, there is an obvious potential problem when you transform yourself into your animal in a public place: people are not likely to understand, at least in this culture. But then, as Castaneda once told me, don Juan had a somewhat similar problem even with his Mexican Indian public. He said don Juan explained that one of the reasons he had given up using the hallucinogenic datura ointment was that Indians had taken to shooting at him when he was jumping over trees. A shaman's lot is not always a happy one.

Remember, guardian spirits are *always* beneficial. They never harm their possessors. And you possess the guardian spirit; it never possesses you. In other words, the power animal is a purely beneficial spirit, no matter how fierce it may appear. It is a spirit to be *exercised,* not exorcised.

CHAPTER 5

The Journey to Restore Power

Shamans have long felt that the power of the guardian or tutelary spirit makes one resistant to illness. The reason is simple: it provides a *power-full* body that resists the intrusion of external forces. From the shamanic point of view, there is simply not room in a power-filled body for the easy entrance of the intrusive, harmful energies known in ordinary reality as diseases.

A power animal or guardian spirit, as I first learned among the Jívaro, not only increases one's physical energy and ability to resist contagious disease, but also increases one's mental alertness and self-confidence. The power even makes it more difficult for one to lie.

Being power-full is like having a force field in and around you, for you are resistant to power intrusions, the shamanic equivalent of infections. From a shamanic point of view, illnesses usually are power intrusions. They are not natural to the body, but are brought in. If you are power-full, you will resist them. Thus possession of guardian spirit power is fundamental to health. Serious illness is usually only possible when a person is dis-spirited, has lost this energizing force, the guardian spirit. When a person becomes depressed, weak, prone to illness, it is a symptom that he has lost his power animal and thus can no longer resist, or ward off the unwanted power "infections" or intrusions.

You may have been quite successful in the experience of dancing your animal. However, as has been discussed, this is no guarantee that you still retain its power, since it may long since have left you. To be absolutely sure that you have a power animal, there are specific techniques to use. One of these is the shamanic journey to the Lowerworld to retrieve a power animal someone has lost.

While shamans most commonly undertake this journey for another person alone, an unusually elaborate version of the method of restoring guardian spirit power occurred among the Coast Salish Indians of western Washington State. There the shamans had the practice of making the journey together as a group. To do this, they formed a "spirit canoe" or "spirit boat" to undertake a journey whose purpose was to regain the guardian spirit of their patient from the Lowerworld.[1] It "was not the soul of a person in the general sense of the word, but rather his guardian-spirit" that was to be restored to the patient.[2] Among the Coast Salish, the guardian spirit is commonly referred to as the *power animal*, as noted earlier.[3]

The Coast Salish are unusual in the elaborateness of their group spirit canoe methods.[4] When a person began to have symptoms of dis-spiritedness, which among the Salish could include the gradual loss of property or wealth, then he might hire half a dozen to a dozen shamans to engage in a task together to recover his guardian spirit by journeying to the Lowerworld.[5]

On an agreed-upon night the shamans formed two imaginary canoes by standing in two parallel rows inside a large house. Beside each shaman was his magical cedar board, stuck into the dirt floor. Each board was decorated with representations of its owner's experiences when he had his first vision of a spirit canoe. Every shaman, in addition, held a pole six to eight feet long with which he paddled or pushed the spirit canoe. The shaman in the bow was the leader, the one in the stern the steerer.

Accompanied by the shaking of rattles, the beating of drums, and singing, the shamans' "souls or minds sank down through the earth," going in a spirit boat "having the power to 'make land into water' wherever they travel" in the Lowerworld.[6] As they journeyed in the spirit canoe, each shaman, beginning with the leader, sang his own guardian spirit song. A large audience of spectators sat around the walls of the house and joined in the singing to help the shamans.[7]

Sometimes spirit canoe journeys among the Coast Salish lasted five or six nights, with the shamans sleeping during the days and resuming in the evenings at the point in the journey where they had stopped at dawn. More often the journey lasted only two nights, the first night being the journey to the land of spirits, and the second night the return. As soon as the shamans succeeded in retrieving the guardian spirit of their patient, they started the return journey. When they had put the guardian spirit back into the patient, he rose and danced.[8]

The Coast Salish spirit canoe is a large-scale, cooperative version of a much more common and simpler shamanic method of restoring power to a patient. In this method, there are only two or three essential participants: the shaman, the person or patient in need of power restoration, and often an assistant to beat the shaman's drum. Some master shamans can do without the aid of a drummer, but such sonic input is usually necessary.

I first learned this method in 1961 while living with the Conibo, whose shamans frequently use this technique in treating illness. Like the Coast Salish shamans, the Conibo journey down into the Lowerworld in a spirit boat, though usually it is a nonordinary river steamboat rather than a nonordinary canoe! In addition, the Conibo crew is formed not by shamans, but by the single shaman, helped by a large crew of spirits.

The use of some kind of spirit or soul boat in the shamanic journey is widespread in the primitive world. It occurs in Siberia as well as in Malaysia and Indonesia, where it is related to the "boat of the dead."[9] Often the spirit canoe is in the form of a serpent, as in aboriginal Australia, or as in the "Snake-Canoe" of the Desana Indians of the South American tropical forest.[10] For other groups, such as the Tapirapé of central Brazil, little is known of the specific form of the spirit canoe used by the shamans.[11] Sometimes a shaman may use a spirit raft, as in Siberia.[12]

More often, shamans undertaking the shamanic journey do not use a canoe or watercraft in the SSC, but employ the same basic method. In other words, they "sink" into the Lowerworld to recover a spirit, but without bothering to create a "canoe" or any other conveyance. For my own part, I usually only conceptualize a canoe when working in the Coast Salish style with a group, even though the boat method was what I was introduced to by the Conibo. Every shaman, as the years go by, should be prepared to modify and adapt his methods in accordance with what seems to work best for him.

The method that I wish to introduce to you is a relatively simple and basic adaptation of the retrieval journey. This same basic technique can be used not only to recover a guardian spirit for another person, but also can be employed, with certain differences, to heal patients by retrieving lost portions of their vital souls. That, however, is advanced work not dealt with here.

One of the important elements in this method is lying down beside the patient on the floor or ground. The falling down or lying down of the shaman beside the patient is a very widespread aspect of the journey method of treatment. One very good reason for this practice is that it is very difficult in a deep SSC to remain standing. But even in a light SSC, the shaman usually wants to lie down in order to *see* and experience the journey clearly by being fully relaxed and not having to be concerned with keeping himself functioning in ordinary reality by having to stand or sit. A Yaralde Australian tribesman eloquently described the need for lying down in doing *seeing:*

> If you get up, you will not see these scenes, but when you lie down again, you will see them, unless you get too frightened. If you do, you will break the web (or thread) on which the scenes are hung.[13]

In the guardian spirit retrieval method taught here, the person in the role of the shaman brings back the power animal and blows it first into the chest of the patient. From the Jívaro I learned that a person's guardian reposes primarily in the chest, although its power emanates throughout the entire body. A Jívaro shaman, taking the *ayahuasca* drink, sees an inverted rainbow in the chest of someone who possesses a guardian. The idea that the guardian resides primarily in the chest is apparently widespread, also occurring, for example, in aboriginal Australia as well as in western North America.[14]

The fontanelle, or so-called "soft spot" location in the top rear of the head where the temporal and occipital bones meet, is an important entrance and exit point for power, and it is for that reason that a shaman, after blowing the guardian spirit into the chest, then blows into the fontanelle of the patient. This is to finish putting in whatever remains of the power he has brought back.

Hunting a Power Song

Before undertaking the shamanic journey to retrieve a power animal, you should acquire a power song. Each shaman has at least one power song that he uses to "wake up" his guardian and other helpers to help him in healing and other work. To get a power song, plan to spend a day alone in a wild natural place, a location where you will not encounter people and where the natural environment has not been too altered by humans. Rasmussen, the great student of Eskimo life, puts it well:

> . . . The best magic words are those which come to one when one is alone out among the mountains. These are always the most powerful in their effects. The power of solitude is great and beyond understanding.[15]

A remote forested or mountainous area is ideal, but if you cannot reach such a place, try to do the best you can. Do not eat breakfast, and fast throughout the day as you quietly stroll and sometimes sit. Do not plan an itinerary; just see where your feet take you. As you wander, discover what animal you feel like. It may or may not be the one you danced. Take on its feelings, and enjoy its identity during the day. As this is your first hunt for a song, you may only encounter the melody.

If so, later, you should find your own words, too. But for now, I give you the words of one of mine that I acquired when I was studying with the Jívaro:

I have spirits,
Spirits have I.
I have spirits,
Spirits have I.
I have spirits,
Spirits have I.
I, I, I.

   (repeat three more times and go to the next stanza)

My spirits
Are like birds,
And the wings
And bodies are dreams.
I have spirits,
Spirits have I.
I, I, I.

   (repeat three more times and return to the first stanza)

Repeat the song as long as you feel that it is needed. A power song also helps one to enter the SSC, both through its words and melody. The more you use the song in shamanic work, the more effective it will be as an adjunct in altering your state of consciousness. Eventually, it can act as a small "trigger" to help you shift into the SSC.

One can also seek a special power song to sing during the journey.

This is best discovered while actually doing a journey and usually involves a description of what one sees. This free adaptation by Cloutier of a Northwest Coast Tsimshian shaman's song is a good example:

I go in my canoe
all over
in my vision

over trees
or in water
I'm floating

all around
I float
among whirlpools

all around
I float
among shadows

I go in my canoe
all over
in my vision

over trees
or in water
I'm floating

whose canoe
is this
I stand in

the one
I stand in
with a stranger

I go in my canoe
all over
in my vision

over trees
or in water
I'm floating[16]

You may also involuntarily acquire a song while you are dreaming. The late Essie Parrish, a Pomo Indian shaman in California, gave this account of dreaming her first power song:

I'm going to tell another story about when I was young—about how I first sang a song when I was a child. I was eleven years old at that time. I didn't acquire that song in any ordinary way—I dreamed it.

One time, as I lay asleep, a dream came to me—I heard singing up in the sky. Because I was little, because I didn't realize what it was, I didn't pay (conscious) attention to it—I just (passively) listened when that man was singing up above. Still he made it known to me—it was as if it entered deep into my chest, as if the song itself were singing in my voice box. Then it seemed as if I could see the man, as if I could just make him out.

After I awoke from sleep, that song was singing inside me all day long. Even though I didn't want to sing, still the song was singing in my voice box. Then I myself tried, tried to sing, and amazingly the song turned out to be beautiful. I have remembered it ever since.

Then, one time, I and my older sister accompanied our grandmother to Danaká. At that time she was little too, but she was bigger than I. We traveled with her (our grandmother). Having descended to Danaká, we lived there.

Then early one morning we went to Madrone Beach to gather seaweed. We accompanied our grandmother. While sitting there on a boulder, we were playing dolls and chattering and laughing. But still that song was always singing deep inside of me. And then because it was singing in my voice box, I too began singing. It turned out that my sister heard me.

"What are you singing?" she asked me. "I'm singing a song," I said. "How beautiful it sounds. Where did you hear that song?" she inquired. "I dreamed it," I replied. When I said that, I felt embarrassed. "Please sing it again," she said. Then I started the song. "Oh, how beautiful it sounds. Teach it to me," she said. I then replied, "It's not for such purposes. It's not for you to learn." Then, because she was bigger than I, she made me sing anyway. Even though I didn't want to sing, she still made me.

Then I sang the song. . . .

"But don't tell this to anyone," I said. "Why?" she asked. "They might make me sing." "All right," she said. That turned out not to be true. We returned home in the evening. My sister, in spite of (what she had promised), told my mother's mother's older brother—he was strange, a silly person. He said, "They say that you have a song." "Well, who said that?" I asked. "Your older sister said that you sang a beautiful song. Please sing it," he said. So I sang again for him. It sounded extremely good to him.

That was the first song that I sang when I was little. I'm going to stop right there.[17]

75

Making the Journey to Recover a Power Animal

Earlier, you learned how to make an introductory journey into the Lowerworld. This new journey is simply a continuation of what you did before, but it is also serious shamanic work. Be sure you have already completed the previous exercises successfully. Study the instructions carefully several times beforehand so that you will remember the steps.

You will need a partner who has also studied the book. In addition, you will require a drum (or a cassette recording of shamanic drumming) and a rattle. If you use a drum, you will also need a third person to do the drumming.*

To restore a power animal to someone, it is not necessary that the person be lacking one. What *is* important is that a power animal "take pity" on the patient, in response to the shaman's request for help during the journey. The intervention of one human being (the shaman) on behalf of another often seems to evoke sympathy in the hidden universe, and usually a former, lost power animal of the patient volunteers to come back with the journeying shaman. Each additional one that returns adds to the spiritual power of the receiver, but he should take care to honor those that return and not be "greedy," or they may leave him again.

This is a journey to bring back a guardian that your "patient" has lost. Since over one's lifetime one may unknowingly or knowingly have the help of a series of different power animals, there is no ordinary way of guessing in advance whether the animal is one your "patient" danced or otherwise might expect to return to him. Power animals normally come and go unexpectedly from a person, especially after a few years. Accordingly, the regular practice of this exercise is an important way for a person to be assured of possessing power. And if a person shows power-loss through depression or illness, and asks for help, such work should be immediately undertaken.

The steps are as follows:

1. Plan with your partner and a third person to spend an evening together. Abstain from alcoholic beverages and mind-altering drugs throughout the day. Eat only a light lunch and no dinner.

2. Use a room free of light and external noises. Clear the area of furniture. Light a candle on the floor in one corner of the room, where it will not throw much light.

* See Appendix A for information on drums and cassettes.

3. The person who is to act as shaman, in this case yourself, should go through all the steps of the *Starting Dance* and *Dancing Your Animal* described on pages 65–67. If you have a drummer, have him beat the drum in time to your rattle, but only when you are actually dancing (see Plate 6).

4. Shake your rattle four times in the six directions (east, north, west, south, up, and down) to catch the attention of the spirits, wherever they may be. Then whistle four times to call the spirits. Next, walk very slowly around the patient four times, shaking the rattle in a slow but strong and steady tempo, and return to stand beside him.

5. Begin to whistle your power song, the song with which you call upon your spirits to help you, shaking your rattle in accompaniment. Whistle this, usually for a few minutes, until you are aware that there is a slight alteration in your consciousness.

Plate 6.   *Beating the drum for the shamanic journey. Drawn by Barbara Olsen.*

77

6. Now begin to actually sing the words, continuing to shake the rattle in the same strong, slow beat.

7. Continue repeating your song until you are aware that your consciousness is altering. With practice and experience one easily recognizes when this light trance is being reached. Some of the more obvious signs are increased tempo of singing and rattling, trembling arms, and even uncontrollable shivering. When the time is right, you will experience an almost irresistible desire to collapse or lie upon the floor next to the patient. Put this off as long as possible, until you cannot resist slumping to the floor.

8. On the floor, push your prone body up against the patient, shoulder-to-shoulder, hip-to-hip, foot-to-foot. Without delay, in the darkness, begin to shake the rattle back and forth just above your chest. When you start shaking your rattle, the drummer begins beating in time with it.

9. Shake your rattle at a rate that is in the range of about 180 times per minute. Lying on the floor, cover your eyes with one forearm to exclude any light from the candle, and maintain the rattling until you clearly see your entrance into the Lowerworld (see Plate 7). (Only you, acting in the role of the shaman, undertake the journey; your partner, acting as the patient, has no responsibility to see or experience anything.)

When you go into the entrance, stop shaking the rattle; but the drummer should maintain the beat strongly at the same tempo you had been using. He should continue to do this at this cadence throughout your journey until you signal him with your rattle four times (Step 14). The beat of the drum is essential to the maintenance of the journey of the canoe. In a sense, the drum *is* the canoe, as the Chukchee of Siberia say.[18] As the drummer maintains the beat:

10. Continue to visualize the entrance or opening into the earth, and then enter it. Follow the cave or Tunnel downward. The passage may appear as a long, ribbed tube; it may appear as a series of caverns; it may be a flowing stream (see Plate 8). Follow it down wherever it goes. Pass around any obstacles that may appear.

11. *Avoid any ominously voracious nonmammals you may encounter in your journey* (the shamanic reasons for this will be explained in Chapter 7). Especially avoid and pass around any spiders or swarming insects, as well as fanged serpents, fanged reptiles, and fish whose teeth are visible. If you cannot pass them, simply return back up out of the Tunnel and try on another occasion. This is true throughout your journey.

Plate 7.   Entrance into the earth. Drawn by Barbara Olsen.

79

Plate 8.   The Tunnel. Drawn by Barbara Olsen.

12. When you emerge from the Tunnel, you will find yourself in the Lowerworld (see Plate 9). It is here, amidst whatever landscapes you see, that you search for a guardian spirit or power animal for your partner. Search, with your eyes still closed, as the sound of the drum supports you in your journey.

13. The secret to recognizing the power animal is a simple one: it will appear to you at least four times in different aspects or at different angles (see Plate 10). It will be a mammal or bird (in which cases it does not matter if it appears menacing), a serpent, other reptile, or fish *(provided that in these last three cases they do not show their fangs or teeth)*. It may even be a ''mythic'' animal or in human form. It is almost *never* an insect.

Do not strain yourself to find the animal. If it is going to make itself available to you to take back for your partner, it will do so. Do not worry as to whether it presents itself to you in a living form, as a sculpture in wood, stone, or other material. All its presentations are valid. Again, do not try too hard. Your search should be relatively effortless, for you are drawing upon power beyond your ordinary self.

14. After seeing the animal four times, clasp it to your chest immediately with one hand. The animal will come willingly; otherwise it would not have presented itself. Clasping the animal in this manner, pick up and sound the rattle sharply four times. This signals the drummer momentarily to stop drumming. Then shake the rattle in a very fast cadence (in the range of 210 times per minute), setting the tempo for the drummer. Return rapidly through the Tunnel to the room. Usually this takes less than thirty seconds. This return journey should be done rapidly, to avoid inadvertently losing the guardian animal.

15. Set the rattle aside, keep the animal clasped to your chest and rise up on your knees, facing your prone partner. (The drummer should stop as soon as he sees you get up on your knees). Immediately place your cupped hands containing the guardian spirit on your companion's breastbone, and blow with all your strength through your cupped hands to send it into the chest of your partner (see Plate 11a). Then, with your left hand, raise your companion to a sitting position, and place your cupped hands on the top rear of your partner's head (the fontanelle). Forcefully blow again to send any residual power into the head (see Plate 11b). Pick up the rattle. Shaking it rapidly and sharply, pass it in a circle four times around the whole length of your companion's body, making complete the unity of the power with the body.

Plate 9.   Emergence into the Lowerworld from the Tunnel. Drawn by Barbara Olsen.

82

Plate 10.   Seeing a power animal four times. Drawn by Barbara Olsen.

83

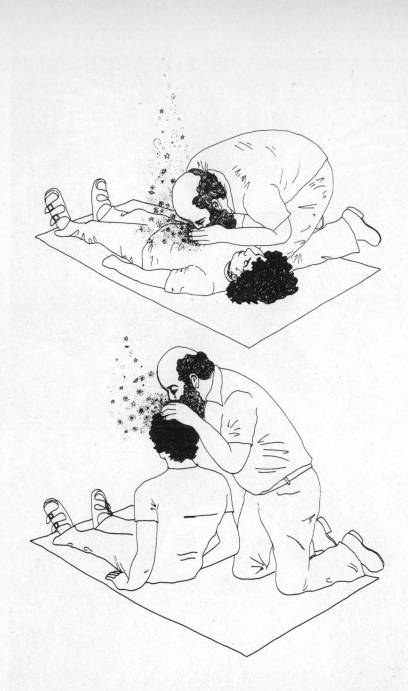

Plate 11.   (a) Blowing the guardian back into the patient's chest. (b) Blowing the guardian back into the patient's head. Drawn by Barbara Olsen.

16. Quietly tell your partner the identity of the animal you brought back. If it is an animal whose name you do not know, then describe the appearance of the creature. Describe all details of the journey.

17. Assist your partner to dance his animal, in order to make the animal feel welcome by giving it the reward of experiencing its movements in material form. As you shake the rattle, gradually increase the tempo in accordance with the patient's movements. The drummer follows the shaman's lead. After just a few minutes, shake your rattle four times, and thereby end the drumming and the dance. Then gently assist the dancer to a sitting position on the floor. Remind him to dance his animal regularly so that it will stay with him.

18. You can now change places with your partner and the same kind of journey can be undertaken for your benefit. When your animal is brought back, you too dance it.

Most Westerners are surprised to discover the vividness and reality of the journey to retrieve a power animal. Apparently, their potentiality for experiencing the shamanic journey and for being *see-ers* is far greater than they expect. If either you or your partner were not successful, don't be discouraged. Try again later. Some of those with the greatest potential are slow starters.

The following free rendition by Cloutier of a Tsimshian song from the Northwest Coast dramatizes the journey to recover a guardian spirit, in this case, Otter:

Ye hey
hyo
ye hey hey
hee

Otter chases
swims straight toward me
Otter's coming
I float off with him

ye hey
hyo
ye hey hey
hee

right beside me
I work my spirit
charm of the opening
beneath all things

ye hey
hyo
ye hey hey
hee

Otter dives in
swims beneath me
there in the opening
beneath all things

ye hey
hyo
ye hey hey
hee

Otter's in me
deep within me
Spirit Otter swimming
in the place beneath me

ye hey
hyo
ye hey hey
hee[19]

Journeys

You may be interested in comparing your guardian spirit retrieval
journey experiences with those of others working with a partner. Here
are a few representative examples from my workshops.

In this first case, the person properly waited until an animal
presented itself four different times. A close-up view of only a portion of
the animal, such as of one eye, is perfectly valid, as long as it is clear
that it is of that particular animal.

I went into the same hole I used earlier this evening. First there was
water. Then the water sort of dropped off, like in locks. I kept jumping off
onto the next one, and the next. The water finally turned into dirt. I was
running along, still in the same cave, but a wooden bridge appeared. Then
I was running across the bridge. It went up at an angle, and at the end
there were stairs. I climbed those stairs for a long time until I finally came
out on what looked like an African plain. There were a lot of different
animals that appeared and disappeared. Finally I saw an antelope was

standing by a waterhole. She immediately became very vivid, very vivid, and appeared four different times. Oh, she was even above me at one time. The last time was a very bold close-up of one eye. So I carried her back here to my partner.

In the next case, the animal gave an unusual exhibition of his power by charging the person twice, even on one occasion running right through him. This is something that commonly happens on vision quests of both North American Plains Indians and of the Jívaro, as well as the experience of "blacking out" afterward, which the person also reported. The individual had not been taught about these matters. The fact that the power animal is a horse is worth noting, for it might appear that this is an exception to the usual rule that domesticated animals cannot serve as guardian spirits. But the horse that appears is a wild one, without a rider and untamed.

I went down into my hole, which is on the side of a cliff on an island I once visited off the coast of Spain. It leads into an underwater cave about ten yards in diameter that you can physically only reach by diving. I was sitting in there waiting for something to happen when a horse started to run at me. You know, if you see a horse running at you it's very scary; so I guess I blacked out. So anyway, when I came to, which was like instantaneously, I saw a white ram where the horse had been. He was moving his head as though to get me to look to the side. I looked around. Behind me I saw this white horse with a brown mane—it was the same one I saw before. He started running at me again. I thought, oh God, here he comes again. He came at me and ran through me. Then I saw this ram again. Well, I had seen the horse twice and the ram twice. So I was looking around and thinking, well, that's twice, I ought to see something four times.

Then I started seeing fish. I saw one like a sailfish go in and out of the water twice. I thought, well, that's twice. So now there were three animals that I had seen twice. Then the fish did it again. So that was three times. Then he dived once more. I looked where I expected he was going to come out, and out came this very ugly catfish. Well, that was not him.

Then this bear started meandering over toward me, but it turned around. It seemed like I moved him away with my own power. Then these wolves were starting to come at me, when suddenly here came the horse. He reared up to protect me from the wolves. So that was three times with the horse. Anyway, he disappeared. So I turned around to look for my way back, and there he was standing right where the hole is. The horse, white with a brown mane. So I brought him back.

Sometimes the shaman does not succeed in his journey to retrieve the power animal for his patient. The following individual's experience illustrates this. Still, every journey adds to the shaman's knowledge and awaits gradual integration with the other information he acquires in the SCC.

> This particular journey was a very strange one for me. It was a journey through a world that was completely uninhabited by anything. The world was entirely artificially constructed, a world that was completely built by humans or other intelligent creatures, all completely chambers and very geometrical. It was somewhat like a super space station, with no sign of any life there at all. It seemed as though there may have been some hidden there, however, in terms of robots.

In the next case, as in the one where the horse was the power animal, the eagle demonstrates its power through visually ferocious behavior.

> I went into this cave I'm familiar with, and just kept going back and back. Then I hit this tunnel and went down through it fast. I just kind of felt where I was going. When I came out I was in the same territory I had visited before. I saw an eagle, but it flew away. Then there was a red squirrel sitting on the tree. I wasn't sure whether the guardian was going to be the red squirrel or the eagle. I waited some time, and then all of a sudden the eagle came back and attacked the squirrel. At first I thought the eagle was going to kill the squirrel and eat it, but it didn't. It stopped attacking. After the squirrel had disappeared, the eagle flew around. I saw it from various angles, and I brought it back.

As I mentioned earlier, the Conibo use the roots of certain trees to descend to the Lowerworld. The person in the following case independently discovered that technique for himself. It is a good illustration of how one accumulates shamanic knowledge, even with regard to method, in the SSC. For brevity's sake, only the initial part of the person's account is presented (the tiger was the power animal for his partner).

> I went down the hole and walked underground alongside the roots of a pine tree. Since the rough ground was uncomfortable, I climbed onto a root and walked down on it. The roots kept branching off, getting thinner all the time. Then I came to the slightly lighter-colored root I had used in the last journey and I branched off onto it. I followed it until it suddenly

stopped. There was a deep well in front of me, all its walls completely black. I realized that I would have to go down, so I jumped right in. I fell for a very long time through darkness until finally I could see the outline of something narrow and straight below. It was a thick rope that was part of a hanging bridge crossing the well. I landed on the rope and let myself down on the bridge. I walked toward the right. As I stepped off the bridge, I saw a magnificent tiger standing to one side and looking at me. . . .

Synchronicities

One of the interesting features of a successful guardian spirit journey is that it often involves synchronicities, or remarkable coincidences. For example, it is common for the patient, after receiving an animal, to reveal to the shaman that he or she already had an unusual connection with that particular animal. It may have been a deep childhood association, a recent peculiar encounter, or a long-time tendency to collect images and drawings of the particular creature.

Another kind of synchronicity that often occurs is that the patient experienced some of the same details of the journey as the shaman, although no verbal communication took place. This kind of similarity in experience is even more dramatic when a large group of persons undertakes the shamanic journey together as the crew of a spirit canoe. Not uncommonly, several members of the crew will encounter the same animal repeatedly and corroborate specific details of its appearance in the discussion at the end of the journey.

In shamanic work it is important to be on the lookout for the occurrence of positive synchronicities, for they are the signals that power is working to produce effects far beyond the normal bounds of probability. In fact, watch for the frequency of positive synchronicities as a kind of homing beacon analogous to a radio directional signal to indicate that the right procedures and methods are being employed.

When "good luck" is surprisingly frequent, the shaman is working correctly and benefiting from power. Here are a couple of representative cases that illustrate the kinds of positive synchronicities that sometimes occur in guardian spirit retrieval work.

In the first case, the person acting as patient saw the power animal as soon as it was blown into him, without being told anything about it by the person acting as shaman.

The partner acting as shaman: I went down into the opening of the earth and down into a tunnel which I've been to many times before. I passed over the small stream that flows through it. This time I went into a dark passageway of the cave that I've never been into before. I had always passed it up and gone another way. Then I came out into a desert place and there were a lot of different forms of cactus around. I saw a variety of the kinds of animals that one sees in the desert. Then I saw a mountain lion. This all happened very fast. The mountain lion kind of ran away from me like it was teasing me, but it did run around in different directions so that I saw it from four different angles. I then brought it back.

The partner acting as patient: Right after he sat me up and blew into my head, immediately I saw a vivid picture of a cat with teeth with mouth wide open, growling. I figured it had to be related because it was just really so vivid. And then he told me that a mountain lion was what he had put into me.

In the next case, Partner A had earlier made an introductory journey of exploration in which he had encountered an old farmhouse and a mountain goat nearby on a hill. He had told no one about this. Then when Partner B (in ignorance of A's experience) took the journey to retrieve a power animal for him, she found a farmhouse and a mountain goat near it on a mountainside. She brought it back for him. This kind of synchronicity means, from a shamanic point of view, that there can be no doubt about his power animal and its willingness to be brought back to him.

Partner A: I just whipped right through the Tunnel. I knew I was going a long way and I was going really fast. I came out at a place that was like a farm. It seemed very old and far away. I kind of stayed around the farm building for a while. Everything was wooden, nothing modern. Then I climbed way up on this hill and saw this goat there, this mountain goat. Then I came back.

Partner B: I went to my cave and down through the hole. I was not feeling very optimistic really about finding anything. Then all of a sudden I noticed up on a ledge was this mountain goat—a white and really pretty goat. He was looking at me. Then he dashed away and up into a meadow. I followed him there. In this meadow was a big farmhouse way out in the distance. It was a really beautiful meadow. When I got up to the farmhouse, I saw the goat again up on the mountainside. I saw the goat four times. The fifth time I saw him, he was getting ready to go down a hole. I wanted to follow him on down because he was playful, but I didn't. I got him and came back.

Partner A: I hadn't told her about seeing the goat. Every time something like this happens my rational mind asks, is this really an experience from outside, or did our subconscious manufacture it? But really, it's a pointless question.

The Group Spirit Canoe

The Coast Salish spirit canoe method, described earlier, can be adapted to serve as a valuable group experience, with a large number of persons joining together to constitute the canoe to retrieve someone's power animal. These persons should all have successfully completed the work up to this chapter, and one of them should already be recognized as a shaman. If you form a group to make a spirit canoe, you should ideally have somebody as a patient who is seriously depressed, dis-spirited, or otherwise ill—someone who is really in need of power, so that you can fully utilize the group effort.

In this adaptation of the spirit canoe method, the shaman lies down beside the patient, as in the usual guardian spirit recovery method. A difference from the prior technique you learned is that the other members of the group join together to form a canoe around the pair and serve as paddlers, polers, lookouts, and protectors in terms of the journey into the Lowerworld.

The basic steps in this adaptation are as follows:

1. All participants, except the patient, should go through the steps of the *Starting Dance* and *Dancing Your Animal* described on pages 65–67. During these dances, have the drummer beat in time to the shaman's rattle. If the participants have rattles, they can shake them, while dancing, in the tempos set by the shaman.

2. The patient lies down on his back on a blanket spread on the floor of a quiet, darkened room. The persons acting as the shamanic crew form the outline of a canoe around the prone patient, with the prow pointing in the same direction as the patient's feet. The members of the crew form the sides of the canoe and are the paddlers. Each keeps in touch with the person in front and behind him with his legs so a human chain is formed without a break.

At the rear of the canoe, in the center of the stern, sits the drummer. Across his knees lies the drum that will provide the beat for the paddlers as the canoe journeys into the Lowerworld (see Plate 6).

91

3. When the paddlers have formed the canoe, the shaman leading the group extinguishes all light except one candle behind the drummer, and steps into the middle of the canoe.

4. The shaman now does the same work as described in Steps 4 and 5 in *Making the Journey to Recover a Power Animal* (page 77).

5. The group accompanies the shaman in singing his power song. Spirit canoe work is more effective if the entire group is singing the words together.

6. The shaman now does the same work described in Steps 6 through 9 in *Making the Journey to Recover a Power Animal* (page 78).

7. Then, at the same time the drum beat begins, the members of the crew begin to paddle. The crew may choose to paddle physically to the beat of the drum, but need not use material poles or paddles. In the darkness of the room, all the participants—the shaman, the drummer, and all the crew members—are visualizing their entrances into the Lowerworld.

The shaman, in the center of the canoe beside the patient, is the only member of the canoe whose mission it is to search for the guardian spirit. It is his responsibility alone. The other members of the canoe crew are, however, engaged in *seeing,* and will search the Lowerworld to repel any perceived dangers and to collect information to share after the journey is over. By having joined in the shaman-leader's power song to call their spirits, they now have with them their own particular guardians. With the aid of these power animals, they will search the Tunnel and then the Lowerworld. If they see any fanged reptile, any voracious insects, or any nonmammalian creatures whose teeth are showing, they are to exhort their own power animals to keep them away from the canoe. In doing so, they may make the sounds of their particular animals.

8. The shaman now undertakes the work described in Steps 10 through 14 in *Making the Journey to Recover a Power Animal* (pages 78, 81).

9. When the shaman shakes his rattle sharply four times to signify that he has the patient's guardian spirit, it is a signal to the drummer and the whole crew that the return journey should be undertaken immediately. They visualize the canoe sharply turning around and returning up through the Tunnel, as they paddle with maximum speed. They and the drummer stop as soon as the shaman ceases shaking his rattle, for this means that the canoe has returned.

10. The shaman undertakes the work described in Steps 15 through

16 in *Making the Journey to Recover a Power Animal* (pages 81, 85).

11. To give the patient room to dance his animal, the members of the canoe crew spread out into a circle and sit facing inward. When the dancing is finished, the shaman gently assists the dancer back down to the floor to rest. He puts his arm around the patient to indicate his continued support, and describes his experience on the journey to the others. Then members of the canoe crew may, in turn, describe their own experiences during the journey. The shaman adds comments, supplementing their personal experiences with his own knowledge.

The shaman now takes the opportunity, insofar as his own knowledge permits, to suggest how the individual experiences relate to the patient and to knowledge of nonordinary reality. Before beginning this discussion, the shaman may ask the patient if he has anything he wishes to say. Not uncommonly, the patient volunteers that the particular animal or other guardian brought back by the shaman played a very important role in the patient's life, especially during childhood.

The spirit canoe need not be only used to retrieve guardian spirits; it can also be used to retrieve vital souls (not dealt with here) and for journeys of exploration. Journeys of exploration do not require the presence of a patient in the middle of the canoe. Under such circumstances the drummer has a key position, and the role is best taken by an experienced shaman. The crew shares experiences after each journey to hasten the personal accumulation of shamanic knowledge.

Through journeys of exploration, the shaman gains spirit helpers (see Chapter 7) and knowledge of how to treat different kinds of illness. In such SSC journeys, he is often guided and instructed by his guardian spirit who takes him to the places of particular kinds of spirits. In the following excerpt from an account by a Tavgi Samoyed shaman of Siberia of his first journey to the Lowerworld, a guardian spirit takes him to a locality where he can learn how to treat mental illness:

We saw nine tents before us. . . . Then it seemed to me we were in the street. We entered the first tent where we found seven naked men and women who were singing all the time while tearing their bodies with their teeth. I became very frightened.

"Now I shall explain this to you, myself, because you will not guess it anyway," said my companion [guardian spirit]: "Originally, seven earths were created and it is through the spirits of these seven earths that (men) lose their minds. Some just start singing, others losing their minds,

93

go away and die; others again become shamans. Our earth has seven promontories with a madman living on each of them. When you become a shaman, you will find them yourself."

"Where can I find them—you have led me to the wrong place"—I thought.

"If I do not lead you to see (the spirits), how could you make magic for the insane?" . . . You must be shown all the ways of diseases."[20]

CHAPTER 6

Power Practice

Shamans differ as to whether it is advisable for one to tell people about the identity of his animal guardian. Among the Jívaro its nature is a most secret matter. To disclose the animal's identity while one still has it, they feel, may cause the guardian to leave the person. Among North American Plains tribes, however, it is not uncommon to hear individuals speaking publicly about their guardian spirits. So I leave the matter to you. For myself, perhaps because of my Jívaro training, I lean to not discussing the identity of power animals. In my workshops, however, where persons are working together in a serious context to help one another, sharing such information confidentially for the purpose of improving shamanic knowledge and power does not normally seem to lead to guardian spirit loss. The Salish Sinkaietk Indians of Washington State reportedly hold a similar view.[1]

Use your guardian animal power in daily life by keeping consciously aware of how you feel. When you feel power-full, then that is the time to overcome some major obstacle in your life or to meet an important challenge. When you feel dis-spirited, try to avoid crises—and do not attempt to help anyone else shamanically.

Consulting a Power Animal

Before proceeding to more advanced work, you should make a number of journeys down into the Tunnel to see your guardian animal and to consult it. This kind of consultation is commonly called "divination" in the anthropological literature. A common reason to consult one's power animal is to obtain advice regarding some personal problem. Another reason is to consult with the power animal concerning the nonordinary cause and treatment of a patient's illness.[2] To consult, simply follow the usual steps you have learned to undertake the journey by yourself. As you become adept at this, you may not need any drumming to assist you into the SSC. At first, however, continue to have a partner act as a drummer-assistant or use a cassette recording of shamanic drumming (see Appendix A).

Even though the guardian's power is with you, the guardian moves around at will, constantly entering and leaving your body. As the Jívaro and other peoples know, the power can even remain with you roughly two weeks without the guardian returning to your body.[3] You may not have to journey far before you see your animal since, more often than not, it is usually close by. Often one's power animal is in the Tunnel or just outside its opening at the other end. When you see your guardian, silently greet it, and keeping it visually before you, pose your question. Most commonly, the power animal will provide its answer by moving its body before you in an unusual way. Other times it may lead you on a journey through portions of the Lowerworld, the experiences of the journey being in the nature of an answer to your question. Whichever way the guardian animal chooses to reply to you, you should try to remember every detail clearly, and then return back up the Tunnel to ordinary consciousness.

The first few times you engage in this work, it is best to keep your question simple, so that it can be answered in a "yes" or "no" manner. This makes it easier to understand the answer, as when the power animal moves in reply before you. When you become more experienced in understanding its "language," the questions can be more complicated. To assist yourself in remembering the details of the information you obtain, I suggest keeping a journal or dictating into a cassette recorder afterwards. This is a good habit with regard to your shamanic work in general.

Do not wait until you have a problem, however, to visit with your power animal through the journey method. It is beneficial simply to see it without posing questions. Positive synchronicities in one's life often occur after such visits. Frequently there are solutions to problems that the person has had on his mind.

Journey Foreseeing

The shamanic journey can also be undertaken, at someone's request, as a kind of preview of what will happen to that person on a planned journey in ordinary reality. This European visitor to the Yurak Samoyed of Siberia reported:

> When I was leaving for my summer journey to Tazorskaya Bay I asked a sorcerer [shaman] in Obdorsk what luck I would have on the journey. He beat his drum and set out, so to speak, for that place, traveling on the clouds. When he came to the Pur River he got a head-ache, and I, too, would fall ill there. His boat tipped over in an eddy at the mouth of the Pur River. The same would happen to me. Finally, farther up the Taz River he came to the *numkympoi*—spirit who "gave light." Thus the journey would end happily for me and I would return safely.[4]

Unfortunately, the writer did not indicate to what degree the shaman's predictions were accurate. This is the kind of information that even sympathetic anthropologists tend to omit from their ethnographic accounts. An exception is Kensinger, a highly regarded anthropologist who lived with the Cashinahua Indians of Peru for years. The Cashinahua, like the Conibo and the Jívaro, frequently take shamanic journeys with the assistance of the *ayahuasca* brew. Kensinger provides this unusual personal testimonial to the accuracy of the information they obtained in journeying:

> Several informants who have never been to or seen pictures of Pucallpa, the large town on the Ucayali River terminus of the Central Highway, have described their visits under the influence of ayahuasca to the town with sufficient detail for me to be able to recognize specific shops and sights. On the day following one ayahuasca party, six of the nine men informed me of seeing the death of my *chai*, "my mother's father." This occurred two days before I was informed by radio of his death.[5]

97

Keeping Power

When a power animal is restored to a person, he usually feels better immediately, and then gradually experiences a power flowing into his body over the next few days. If this is your good fortune, do not allow yourself to become complacent. You should begin a weekly routine to retain the power by keeping your power animal content, for the spirit has entered your body not only to help you, but also to help itself. You gain its power; it gains the joy of again experiencing life in a material form. Therefore each week you should devote a few minutes to dancing your animal, with the aid of rattles, as you learned earlier. Persons who maintain the weekly dancing encourage their guardian spirits to stay with them. If this practice is not maintained, then they may not keep the power for long. Those who maintain the weekly routine of exercising their animal report they tend to retain a sense of optimism and power. They commonly say that they are able to deal positively with the problems of daily existence, to be ill infrequently, and to feel physically and mentally healthier.

Even if you dance and exercise your power animal, you may expect it gradually to grow restless and to start traveling long distances when you are sleeping, to wander through the night. The power remains with you even though the guardian is temporarily away. As the Salish Sinkaietk say, "Power is with a person all the time, but the spirit can go far away."[6] If you start waking up in the middle of the night depressed and dis-spirited, however, it indicates your guardian is not just wandering, but has left you.

A restless power animal develops an increasingly weaker and infrequent connection with you. Perhaps you have read that in many primitive cultures people believe that one can become seriously ill or even die from being suddenly shocked or frightened. From a shamanic view, this can happen especially when your animal guardian has a tenuous connection with you. A restless guardian spirit can be jolted out of you, never to return.

Since one's guardian spirit, or even one's soul, can be off wandering while one is asleep, great care is often taken in primitive cultures to awaken persons gently. Thus, among such widely separated shamanic cultures as the Murngin of Australia and the Warao of South America, it is commonly considered dangerous to be wakened suddenly.[7] The Murngin apparently view this as a danger in the daytime as well as

98

night: "During the hot afternoon the men frequently sleep in the shade, and if it becomes necessary to waken one of them, this is never done hurriedly but with great gentleness and care. . . ."[8] In Jívaro houses, people are awakened as gently as possible, often by someone playing soft, beautiful flute music. Needless to say, the use of an alarm clock is not shamanically healthy. In fact, sometimes it is customary not to wake sleeping shamans at all.

The shamanic treatment of shock or fright involves the journey to restore power. For example, if a person was in an automobile accident that was traumatic, a shaman would treat that person regardless of whether the victim was physically injured. Such work, of course, supplements rather than replaces orthodox medical treatment. The specific treatment, if the victim is not in a coma, is to recover or obtain his guardian spirit to re-energize him. If the victim is comatose, the treatment first involves the recovery of his vital spirit or soul (an advanced technique not dealt with here), so that he will not die. The old phrase in English, "to be frightened to death," possibly is a survival of the earlier European shamanic knowledge of such matters.

When one loses a guardian spirit, this does not mean that its power is also sent away immediately. As the Jívaro say, "Its power is like perfume," and lingers, slowly dissipating over a period of several weeks. Early during this time one should seek assistance from a partner to restore another power animal. If this is done right away, the replacement animal may "lock in" the lingering power of the previous one. Thus a person using this technique can gradually, over the years, acquire some of the protective power of a number of guardian spirits. However, the accumulated power will remain "locked in" only as long as a person has at least one power animal in his possession.

Big Dreams

Dreams, from a shamanic point of view, are of two types: ordinary dreams; and nonordinary, or "big" dreams. Shamans are normally only concerned with big dreams. A big dream is one that is repeated several times in the same basic way on different nights, or it is a one-time dream that is so vivid that it is like being awake, an unusually powerful dream. Big dreams are usually communications from your guardian spirit, your power animal. Sometimes the guardian itself appears in the big dream, sometimes not.

Big dreams are to be taken as literal messages, not to be analyzed for hidden symbolism. For example, if you have a big dream that you are injured in an automobile accident, that is a warning for you from the guardian spirit that such an accident will occur. You may not be able to prevent it, but you can enact it symbolically by yourself or with a friend in a very minor way and may thereby prevent its serious occurrence. In other words, the dream is not symbolic, but your enactment of it is. You can easily do this in your home, particularly if you have a shaman partner to help you enact it so that no one gets hurt. Just recreate the dream in a simple, harmless way, and get it over with. This is a technique once known to some tribes in northeastern and western North America.[9]

While on the subject of automobile accidents, here is a report I received from a person shortly after she had learned about "big dreams" as a participant in one of my workshops:

Not long after having attended the workshop, I had an extremely strong dream one night depicting a car accident with me in the car. Upon examining the picture and all my emotions within that dream, I saw I was not badly hurt—mostly shaken by the experience. One vivid feature of the dream accident was that I hit metal twice.

I was aware—at that time—that I was to enact the dream to prevent the reality of the crash on this plane of consciousness. However, being a tester, I consciously chose to do no further activity related to the dream.

About a month later, as I was driving in the car along with my son— being aware of how very warm, loving, and positive we were feeling with each other, a car materialized in front of us an instant before the accident. While waiting for the car to stop its 180-degree spin, I was aware of being pinned against my son within the car by the momentum of the spin, and being outside and slightly over the car watching the entire "dream" taking place—again. During the entire episode I was aware of a feeling of deep peace and the awareness that my guardian spirit was right there with me and shielding me from "danger."

When the car came to a slamming stop I was able to direct the necessary operations with a totally cool head—checking for injuries to myself and my son—being sure the ambulance had been called— reassuring the startled onlookers that all was okay—asking one reliable man to check my son who seemed to be in a mild state of shock. All this was done while I was also checking my own heart beat—shock condition—and positioning my gashed knee over the back of the seat until I could be removed from the car and have it attended to at the hospital.

There was only one aspect of the dream accident that was different

100

from the physical accident: I was on a different street. Also, my dream had shown no other person other than myself.

At first I thought the woman in the other car had hit our car. Upon further investigation I discovered my car had smacked into hers when she drove in front of us. My spinning was also halted by bumping into the back of her car. All things being literal, I did smash into metal and completed the accident by hitting metal again.

Although three human beings were "involved" in the accident, I was the only one to receive a physical injury—that being the deep gash in my knee.

An interesting awareness has come from this accident: I was not seriously hurt and I have only a scar to remind me to enact out any further dreams of a serious nature immediately! There is one further aspect of this entire thing which "fits." When you earlier recovered my guardian spirit, it had something about it denoting material wealth. The scar on my knee—although not at all painful to me—has been considered by the insurance people to be "bad" enough to award me a very sizable amount of money . . . enough that I now feel "wealthy."

You may get a big dream that is good; not at all ominous. This can be taken as a communication from your guardian that it wants to experience the pleasant occurrence in the dream by your actually doing it physically. As with a "bad" big dream, it should be enacted as soon as possible. Of course, in the case of a "good" big dream, you do not have to restrict yourself to only a symbolic enactment.

Guardian spirits are only good; but if your power animal's messages are ignored, or if it is not exercised through dancing, it may become discomforted, discouraged, and want to leave your body. Its discomfort may unintentionally flow into your own consciousness, causing tension and anxiety. If you do nothing to remedy the situation, it will shortly leave you, and you will again be dis-spirited.

Restoring Power at a Distance

The Jívaro are of the opinion that a person possessing a guardian spirit is virtually immune to death, except for that resulting from epidemic disease. Nor can he or she become seriously injured or seriously ill, except, again, in the case of epidemics. It is not clear how many primitive peoples hold a similar view, but the Jívaro assumption about this capability of the guardian spirit cannot be proven or disproven by any standards of ordinary reality. From the Jívaro viewpoint, if a person

101

dies, it is evidence that he had already lost the guardian. Since in ordinary reality, there is no way to interview dead people to ask them if indeed they had lost their guardian spirits before death, one can argue against the Jívaro view only as a matter of belief.

Because of the protective power of the guardian spirit, a person will not be seriously injured or become seriously ill unless he has already lost it. Naturally, then, the urgent healing work of the shaman in such cases is to restore one of the person's lost guardian spirits as soon as possible. Since ours is not a shamanic society, it is usually not possible to do the necessary work in the same room as a hospitalized person. Exceptions are sometimes tolerated in this country if both the shaman and the patient are American Indians. In fact, in some hospitals, such as on the Navaho reservation, visits by native healers are being increasingly encouraged as the Western medical staff becomes more aware of the benefits produced. For non-Indians, however, it may be a long time before shamanic supplementary treatment is accepted in hospital settings. Meanwhile, however, you can use the following long-distance technique to restore guardian power.

Suppose a friend or relative is in a hospital room many miles away, and you would like to help him shamanically. If the person is in serious condition, he probably has lost his guardian spirit. In a quiet, dark room, close your eyes, sing your power song to yourself silently or aloud, and use your rattle, if you have it. Mentally call upon your power animal to wake up, to get active, to help you.

In the darkness, face the direction of the town or place where the person is located, cover your eyes with your hands, and visualize the patient in detail lying on his bed. Working at a distance, for healing or any purpose, requires considerable concentration and clarity of "seeing," as reported for the Australian aborigines.[10] Once you have visualized the person, then go off on the journey to the Lowerworld to recover a power animal for that person. When you recover his power animal, send it, mentally and emotionally, to the patient as visualized in the hospital room.

Now, still with your eyes closed, call upon *your* power animal. When you feel its force strongly around you, send some of its power into the *patient's guardian* to activate it into dancing. Keep this up until you clearly see the patient's power animal get up and start jumping, dancing, or running, around and over the visualized prone patient. It can be done at any distance. Of course, this sounds crazy in OSC terms, and certainly does not fit any model of psychological suggestion. But the positive synchronicities of recovery associated with this method are indeed remarkable. After the patient recovers, ask him if he had dreams or visions of any particular animal. You may be surprised, as I often have been, by what he tells you he independently experienced.

Be careful, when you send power from your power animal to help another person, to send the power only to his animal. Do not send it directly to the person himself, because this might cause damage. Let the power safely filter through his own guardian, which is the only power animal that can be of direct help. *Also, avoid sending your* own *energy to help another person.* You will exhaust yourself and, importantly for the person you wish to help, you will find it hard to continue working. Instead, draw always on your guardian's power. If you do this, you will finish a healing session more energetic than ever, not tired.

As long as the patient remains in critical condition, repeat the process of visualizing his power animal over his prone body every few hours. If you see the animal is just lying there, not alert, not doing anything, then it is a dangerous situation for the patient. You must re-energize it with your own guardian power, as you did before, until it is again running, jumping, or dancing over and around the patient. Not uncommonly, one has to do this every few hours for several days, until the patient is definitely out of danger. Even then, it is desirable to keep up the work once a day. Later, if you think the person would be sympathetic to shamanic work, visit him, explain what you have been doing, and suggest that he himself visualize the animal and mentally "dance" it in his room, while lying in his bed. I have been continually surprised to discover how many Westerners who are ill or injured immediately accept the possibility of their power animal and happily enter into contact with it.

The Bone Game

Power practice includes various contests and games, some more difficult and advanced than others. For persons still new to shamanism, but by no means limited to them, a particularly good one is that known by western North American Indians by such names as the bone game, the stick game, or the hand game. It may be played by only two individuals, but more commonly there are two opposing teams of at least a half a dozen members each. In the game, the teams take turns attempting to *see* the location of a marked bone or bones being hidden by the opposing team. A person designated as the team's "see-er" or "pointer" tries to locate the marked bone(s) within the hands of the opposing team, while the opposing team tries to prevent the pointer from seeing the bones they have hidden.

Shamanic power and seeing are seriously utilized in the bone game. For example, in the Coast Salish area of western Washington State, where the game is still extremely popular, shamans (locally called "Indian doctors" in English) are recognized as the best see-ers. Because of the doctors' power, it is considered presumptuous for others to play against them. As one Salish said:

> They have a powerful mind, it's no use playing when them Indian Doctors are there . . . they just look at you and read what side you got it on right now and that's it . . . that's not just guessing, this is knowing, you see, you can't fool them.[11]

Among the Paviotso or Northern Paiute of Nevada, a man might even seek a vision in a cave at night to obtain power in *seeing* in the game. According to a Paviotso, if the vision comes, thereafter, it is said, "he can see through anything."[12]

Before beginning the game, it is important to have a significant wager agreed upon between the two teams so that the participants will be very serious in using their powers to see or prevent seeing. In the old days, among the western North American Indian peoples, bands or villages playing against one another commonly wagered very heavily. For example, a group might bet its entire winter food supply as the stake. Other groups or individuals might bet their horses or even their wives.

In games in my workshops, the wagers are much less extreme. The opposing teams very frequently agree to the following types of stakes: for example, members of the team that loses will give a half-hour massage to the members of the winning team, or the losing team may prepare a feast for the winning team. There are many possibilities, and one is continually impressed by the innovations that are introduced by participants.

To arrange the wager, someone acts as a master of ceremonies to coordinate the betting. His first act is to divide the group in half. If people are sitting in a circle, this can be simply done by assigning the people on the left half of the circle to one team, and the people on the right to the other. Each team ideally should have an equal number of participants.

104

The master of ceremonies then advises each group to withdraw out of earshot of the other team, so that their discussions cannot be overheard. In their isolated positions, each group discusses what wager it is prepared to lose and what wager it might accept if it wins. The wagers need not be the same. The master of ceremonies shuttles between the two groups, transmitting their offers and counter-offers. He also has the duty of clarifying the rules of the game and arbitrating in case of misunderstandings between the teams.

The process of negotiation can be extremely lengthy, but also a great deal of fun. The protracted period of negotiation heightens the sense of expectation preparatory to the bone contest and is a valuable feature of the exercise. When, through the master of ceremonies, the two teams agree on the wagers, each can begin to prepare for the competition.

All team members are forbidden to talk once the actual confrontation is made, in two opposing lines, to begin the game. Therefore it is important that the teams discuss and work out their tactics and strategy beforehand. In other words, after agreeing on the wagers, each of the teams spends some time working out their plans. Among the things that they do is to select their first *pointer* or see-er, and possibly also back-up pointers in case the first one is not successful. Picking a pointer and back-up pointers who are probably good at seeing is an important part of the deliberations.

Secondly, a first *hider* and back-up hiders have to be selected. A team may prefer to wait until the game really gets going before selecting back-up pointers and hiders, since it may be only then that people sense their abilities to see and hide. Since talking is not allowed by members of either team after the actual game begins, nonverbal communication will have to be used to indicate whether someone is volunteering to be a new see-er or hider.

The master of ceremonies should explain to the teams that the best see-ers often work with their eyes closed, for they are working shamanically. Some see-ers are even best when they turn their backs to the opposing team and work that way. Other see-ers indeed work with their eyes open. They learn through experience what is best for them individually.

The teams must also decide on how they will help in the seeing process. They may, for example, decide to touch all their bodies together as a group leading to the see-er, to try to create a "cone" of power. The team members are also instructed to try to disrupt the concentration of the see-er when their own side is hiding the bones.

They can scream, shout, dance, make the noises of their power animals, and whatever else they wish to do to disconcert the pointer on the opposing team.

Prior to beginning the game, the teams may decide to sing power songs to help themselves develop their awakening of spirits, but after the game begins, no songs involving words are allowed. This does not, however, prohibit using songs with no human words. In fact, part of the practice of the bone game is to use your animal aspect consciously.

When both teams are ready to play, they line up facing each other, about four feet apart. If outdoors, the master of ceremonies draws a line in the dirt between them. If indoors, the line can be a cord or a row of candles (see Plate 12). It is against the rules for any part of a team member's body, including his hands, to cross over the center line. If such an infraction occurs, the master of ceremonies, acting as referee, then awards a *counter* to the opposing team.

Counters may be (indoors) turkey feathers laid on the floor, or (outdoors) sticks stuck into the ground. Such sticks, usually painted with the particular colors of a team, are eight to ten inches in length,

Plate 12.   The Bone Game. Drawn by Barbara Olsen.

pointed at one end, and about the thickness of pencils. About three or four counters on each side are usually sufficient for a short game. Each team lays out its counters on its own side of the line.

The objective of the game is to win all the counters. A team has to win not only the other team's counters but also its own counters, a concept somewhat different from European games. In other words, if each team puts out, let us say, three counters, then each team has to win first the other team's three counters and then its own three counters in order to win the game. It is important for the referee to take the responsibility for keeping track of these counters and for lifting them over the line between the two teams.

In this relatively simple adaptation of the hand game, only two *bones* are used. The two bones or sticks are slightly shorter than the breadth of a person's palm, and frequently are chicken wing bones, or dowels half an inch in diameter. These bones or sticks should be as similar to each other as possible except for one feature: around the center of one is wrapped a binding of black string. The wrapping serves to distinguish between the two bones or sticks of the pair.

The business of hiding is done as follows: the hider turns his back to the opposing team and shuffles the two bones between his hands so as to prevent the opposing team from knowing which hand contains the bone wrapped with string; or the hider may shift the bones back and forth between his hands under a blanket or other cloth on his lap while facing the opposing team; or the hider may toss the bones back and forth between his hands behind his back as he faces the opposing team.

Finally the hider simply sticks his two fists, each one containing a bone, straight out from his body toward the opposing team. This signifies that the hider and his team are ready to have the other team attempt to guess the location of the bone with the string around it. From this point on, no movement of the bones is allowed, in this adaptation of the game.

When the hider has stretched out his fists, then his team begins to engage in all sorts of disruptive shouts and activity, and the master of ceremonies should simultaneously beat a drum in a steady tempo. When he begins to drum it is the signal that pointing is starting. When he stops drumming, it is the signal that the pointer has indicated which hand contains the marked bone.

The team with the see-er remains quiet, concentrating upon providing a shield of tranquility around the see-er as well as power to help him point correctly. When the see-er points towards one of the hider's

107

hands, the master of ceremonies has the hider open that hand. If, on the first attempt, the see-er correctly points to the hand concealing the marked bone, then the pointer's team wins one of the opposite team's counters. It is placed on the winners' side of the line. If the see-er is unsuccessful, then his team loses its turn but does not give up a counter to the opposing team. In other words, counters can only change sides by successful pointing, not by unsuccessful pointing. As long as a team is successful it continues having turns, without interruption. The team that wins all the counters wins whatever wager was staked by the opposing team and agreed upon previously.

There exist many regional and tribal variations among western North American Indians in playing the game.[13] The foregoing was a simplified composite adaptation for beginners. If you wish to advance to a more elaborate bone game, employing four bones, see Appendix B for the version played by the Flathead Indians of Montana.

Power Objects and the Quartz Crystal

As you walk in the woods or in other wild places, keep on the lookout for objects to include in a medicine bundle. Objects that attract you for no clear conscious reason may, from a shamanic point of view, be power objects whose spiritual aspect can be revealed to you in the Lowerworld through the journey. You may in fact have been collecting power objects for many years without knowing it. What about that rabbit's foot of your childhood? And the unusual pebble you found on the seacoast, the feather you picked up in a mountain meadow? These are all possible power objects, objects with power-full associations and memories.

A shaman may group such objects together in a power or "medicine" bundle. He especially includes objects encountered during powerful personal experiences connected with shamanic work. If you have a visionary experience or sense power at a particular location, look about you and see if something distinctive is lying there for you to put into your bundle.

Many shamans keep their power objects, their "medicine," in a wild animal skin. Some keep them in a cloth bag, a leather pouch, or even an old cardboard box. A medicine bundle is something that a shaman normally keeps wrapped up, unwrapping or unrolling it publicly only on ritual occasions. The objects inside are highly personal and, as with other matters of power, it is not good to show them off or talk too much about them; this verges on boasting, and may result in power loss. When the shaman unwraps his medicine bundle and handles the power objects, they are mnemonic—they rekindle in his memory the shamanic experiences to which they are related.

Almost any small object can be included in the medicine bundle. Like other things in shamanism, these decisions are your own. Only you know what is significant for you in terms of your own personal power experiences. Open the bundle and privately review the memories of its contents regularly, especially when about to do shamanic work. If any particular object no longer evokes a power-full memory and emotion for you, return it to a place of dignity in Nature. It is no longer needed.

While there is potentially an almost infinite variety of power objects, there is one kind in particular that is regularly found in the keeping of shamans. This is the quartz crystal. In North and South America, Australia, southeast Asia, and elsewhere, shamans ascribe a singular importance to these pointed, six-sided stones that are usually transparent to milky-white. (They can be seen in the Tunnel wall in Plate 8). Shamans use a wide variety of sizes, ranging from the length of a little-finger joint to rarer ones a foot or more in length.

The quartz crystal is considered the strongest power object of all among such widely separated peoples as the Jívaro in South America and the tribes of Australia.[14] Peoples as distant from one another as the aborigines of eastern Australia and the Yuman-speakers of southern California and adjacent Baja California consider the quartz crystal "living," or a "live rock."[15] The widespread employment of quartz crystals in shamanism spans thousands of years. In California, for example, quartz crystals have been found in archaeological sites and prehistoric burials dating as far back as 8,000 years.[16]

The quartz crystal is, like other power objects, viewed as a spirit helper, whether in Australia or in the Upper Amazon.[17] Jívaro shamans recognize that the quartz crystal is in a class of its own among spirit helpers, not only because of its power but also because it always appears the same to the shaman whether he is in the SSC or the OSC. In other words, its material and spiritual natures are the same. The western Yuman shamans enter into a special partnership with their quartz crystals and must "feed" them; this is reminiscent of Jívaro shamans feeding their spirit helpers with tobacco water in order to keep them.[18]

Quartz crystals are in a sense "solidified light" involved with "enlightenment" and *seeing*. For example, a phenomenon not unlike the "third eye" concept occurred among the Australian Wiradjeri. Shamans in training had a piece of quartz "sung" into their foreheads so that they would "be able to see right into things."[19] Also in Australia, quartz crystals were often pressed or scratched into the skin of such trainees, or rubbed over their bodies, to give them power, and among the Wiradjeri "liquefied quartz" was poured over their bodies.[20] Among the Wiradjeri, quartz crystals were put into water for shaman trainees to drink, so that they "could see ghosts."[21] In South America, the pebbles within a Warao shaman's rattle are quartz crystals, spirit helpers that assist him in extracting harmful intrusions from patients.[22] At death the Warao shaman's soul merges with the quartz crystals inside his rattle and ascends to the sky in the form of light.[23] The association of quartz crystals with the sky and celestial phenomena is a significant one, connected not only with light but with the sun. A Mexican Huichol shaman's soul may return to earth from its celestial abode in the form of a quartz crystal,[24] and a beginning Huichol shaman may take a journey to the sky to retrieve such a crystal from behind the sun.[25]

In native Australia, the quartz crystal is associated likewise with the sky and may be found by a shaman at the foot of the rainbow where it ends in a body of water.[26] The Australian Kabi or Wakka shaman "with many crystals in his body" could journey down into the deepest water holes, where the rainbow spirit lived, and receive more quartz crystals. Such a shaman would arise "full of life, and be a medicine-man of the highest degree."[27]

One might assume that the quartz crystal is considered powerful simply because it is a transparent rock, but so is mica, and the latter is rarely, if ever, referred to in the shamanic literature. This suggests that something more than transparency is involved. It might be the fact that quartz crystals sometimes can refract light to show rainbow-like colors. But is that sufficient explanation for its unique importance as an object involved in the shamanic manipulation of *power?* The answer may lie in a most curious coincidence. In modern physics the quartz crystal is also involved in the manipulation of power. Its remarkable electronic properties early made it a basic component in radio transmitters and receivers (remember the crystal set?). Thin wafers sliced from quartz crystals later became basic components for modern electronic hardware such as computers and timepieces. While this all may be coincidental, it is one of the many synchronicities that make the accumulated knowledge of shamanism exciting and often even awesome.

Shamans have long used their quartz crystals for *seeing* and divination. Not surprisingly, bone game players sometimes carry a quartz crystal for luck.[28] The crystal ball with which people in our culture are familiar, at least by name, is simply a polished descendant of the old shamanic crystal. Among the Yualai (Euahlayi) of Australia, the best shamans practiced crystal-gazing to "see visions of the past, of what is happening in the present at a distance, and of the future."[29] Both the Yualai and the distant Tsimshian of the Northwest Coast of North America sent the quartz crystal or its spirit to fetch the image of a particular person. This technique was even used among the Tsimshian to effect long-distance healing. The shaman sent out the crystal at night to bring back the image of the sick person. When the image arrived, the shaman danced around the crystal, shaking his rattle (presumably entering the SSC), and then ordered the crystal, as his spirit helper, to extract a harmful power intrusion from the image. The distant person, whose image it was, was thereby healed.[30]

The shaman normally carries his quartz crystals concealed from other persons and from the rays of the sun. The Jívaro shaman keeps them in his monkey-skin shoulder bag, along with other power objects, green tobacco leaves, and a small gourd cup for steeping the leaves in cold water. The Australian aborigine shaman similarly keeps his quartz crystals in his bag, along with other power objects.[31] He may also keep them in his stomach, the way a Jívaro shaman often keeps spirit helpers.[32] The Tsimshian shaman may carry a quartz crystal in a pouch hanging from his neck.[33] The present-day Paipai (western Yuman) shaman may keep his quartz crystal in a small deer-skin pouch or in a trouser pocket. He depends on it for advice to such a degree that, in his case, it may function more like a guardian spirit than simply a spirit helper. A Paipai shaman stated:

> When you carry that in your pocket, in your dreams it tells you everything, that *wii'ipay* [quartz crystal]. It tells you what you are going to do, what you ask it. And it gives you everything. You need to carry it in your pocket. Yes, if you want to be a [shaman] then you must do this.[34]

Among the western Yuman-speakers of southern California and adjacent Mexican Baja California, specialized techniques are used to locate and extract quartz crystals from their matrices in the landscape.[35] Castaneda similarly refers to special techniques for this purpose in Mexico.[36]

When you start your own medicine bundle, it is desirable to acquire at least one quartz crystal to put into it. Such crystals are the center of power in many shamans' medicine bundles or kits. Their power diffuses through the bundle and helps to energize and maintain the living aspect of the power objects.

The easiest way to begin is to visit mineral supply stores until you find a small quartz crystal that particularly attracts you. Do not immediately put the crystal you choose into your bundle or with your other power objects. First you must cleanse it, since its history is unknown to you. Cleanse the crystal by washing it in the water of a natural spring or the ocean. Then keep it separate from your medicine bundle until the arrival of a winter or summer solstice. Take it to an isolated high place, such as a mountain top. There split a stick at one end, push the unsplit end into the ground, and place the quartz crystal, point upward, in the cleft of the stick. Leave it there eight days in the sun to "re-charge" before putting it in the medicine bundle.

Periodically between solstices, you should remove the crystal from the bundle and "wake up" its power. This is done by hitting its nonpointed end lightly on a rock protruding from a spring or an ocean.

Some central California Indian shamans possessed very large "parent" quartz crystals that were considered especially powerful. Among the Coast Miwok of California, as I had occasion to observe many years ago, a parent crystal was "waked up" in a manner similar to what I have described, but by striking it as hard as possible on a specific rock a few feet offshore in the Pacific Ocean.[37] In the case of such a large quartz crystal the forceful striking was a dangerous procedure; according to the lore of the tribe the world would end if the crystal shattered. This may seem a very farfetched belief to Westerners, but "ending the world" (this is not the same as Castaneda's "stopping the world"[38]) may have been a very accurate description of what would have happened on an individual level. The shaman may have been in danger of ending the world for himself, which after all amounts to the same thing from his point of view. But how? A well-known physicist, David Finkelstein, on hearing of this belief, remarked that the death of the shaman would have been quite possible. He stated that striking such a large quartz crystal a smashing blow theoretically could release hundreds of thousands of volts, or sufficient energy to electrocute the medicine man.[39] Western science has obviously advanced to the point that it recognizes the quartz crystal as a power object, something that shamans have known for thousands of years.

CHAPTER 7

Extracting Harmful Intrusions

The shaman uses the power offered to him not only by the animals, but also by the plants of garden Earth. All of these, of course, derive their power from the sun. While the animals usually act as guardian spirits, the plants tend to serve as spirit helpers. Unlike guardian spirits, spirit helpers are only possessed by shamans. Nonshamans do not normally have the plant power at their disposal.

Just as the powerful guardian spirit animals are usually wild, untamed species, similarly the vast majority of spirit helpers are wild, undomesticated species of plants. It appears that most of the domesticated animals and plants simply do not have the spiritual power necessary to be of significance in shamanism. From a shamanic point of view, the very fact that certain animals and plants have been tamed and domesticated for food and other forms of exploitation is symptomatic of their lack of power.

Plant Helpers

The plant helpers individually do not have nearly as much power as the power animals, but a shaman can come to possess hundreds of spirit helpers, so that their cumulative power can in many ways match that of his guardian spirit. But the importance of the wild plants lies in the variety of their individual capabilities. These plant helpers have two realities, their ordinary and their nonordinary aspects. The nonordinary nature of the plant may be an insect form, for example, a giant butterfly, or some other kind of zoomorphic, or even inanimate, form.

Most of us in our Western "civilization," unlike our ancient ancestors, are sadly ignorant of the identities of wild plants. Accordingly, for many of us, the accumulation of spirit helpers requires acquiring some elementary knowledge of the properties of particular wild plants, the kind of knowledge that is routinely known among primitive peoples. Here is how I suggest you get your first spirit helper. The technique is the same for your later ones.

First, walk through an area of forest, prairie, desert, or any other undomesticated area. As you stroll through the wild area, keep conscious your mission: to encounter a plant to be your helper. When one plant seems particularly to attract you, sit down with it and become familiar with its details. Explain that you have to take all or part of it for your work, and apologize to it before picking part of it or pulling it up. If it is a bush or tree, you may need only pick part of a branch, enough to permit botanical identification. For a smaller plant, you may need an entire flowering specimen. *Take the specimen to someone who will be able to identify it and tell you whether it is poisonous or not.* A knowledgeable farmer or rancher may be able to give you the information; or you can go to a local museum or herbarium for assistance.

Once you know that the species is nonpoisonous, return to the same habitat and find a living member of the same species, apologize to it, and without destroying it eat four small pieces, such as bits of its leaves. Then wrap two more pieces of it together, and put them in your medicine bundle for a later use that will be explained.

Now you are ready to discover its hidden, nonordinary aspect. The evening of that same day, and aided by the sound of drumming, make the shamanic journey into the earth and search until you see two or more of that kind of plant. Visit with the plants, just as you did in the OSC earlier in the day. Keep studying the plants until they change into a nonplant spirit form. Almost any form is possible, but insects, serpents, birds, and even stones are common. As soon as you see the change, eat them in their nonmaterial form in the SSC just as you ate their ordinary material aspect that day; but this time take in the *whole*

114

entity of each of the pair. Then return from the journey. Repeat the whole procedure to acquire each new pair of spirit helpers.

While this work is an adaptation of my Jívaro training, the basic method is also reported from elsewhere in the shamanic world. For example, the way in which plants reveal their hidden nature and make themselves available to the shaman is illustrated by this account of a journey to the Lowerworld by a Siberian Tavgi Samoyed shaman:

> Going along the shore I saw two peaks; one of them was covered with bright-colored vegetation, the other was black earth all over. Between them, there appeared to be an islet with some very nice red plants in blossom on it. They resembled the flowers of the cloudberry. "What is this," I thought. There was nobody near me, but I found it out myself. When a man dies, his face becomes blue and changes: then the shaman has nothing more to do. As I noticed the red grass grew upwards, the black downwards. Suddenly I heard a cry: "Take a stone from here!" The stones were reddish. Since I was marked out to survive, I snatched a red stone. What I thought to be flowers were stones.[1]

In order to use spirit helpers in healing, you should work toward accumulating at least a dozen plants as a minimum. You should probably have among them, in their nonordinary aspects, at least one of each of the following as helpers: Spider, Bee, Yellow Jacket, Hornet, Snake. The greater the variety as well as number of his spirit helpers, the more capable a shaman is of dealing with illness.

The shaman uses spirit helpers in healing persons suffering from harmful power intrusions. The extraction of these intrusions is a more advanced and difficult form of shamanic healing than guardian animal retrieval. *I recommend that you enter such work only if you have already mastered the shamanic journey and guardian spirit work, have acquired the plant helpers, and are extremely serious about shamanism.* As Eliade correctly observes, "in order to extract the evil spirits from the patient, the shaman is often obliged to take them into his own body; in doing so, he struggles and suffers more than the patient himself."[2]

Removing Intrusions

Illness due to power intrusion is manifested by such symptoms as localized pain or discomfort, often together with an increase in temperature, which (from a shamanic point of view) is connected with the energy from the harmful power intrusion. In some ways, the concept of power intrusion is not too different from the Western medical concept of infection. The patient should be treated both for the ordinary aspect of an intrusion (i.e., infection, by orthodox material medicine), and for the nonordinary aspect by shamanic methods.

Power intrusions, like communicable diseases, seem to occur most frequently in urban areas where human populations are the most dense. From an SSC viewpoint, this is because many people, without knowing it, possess the potentiality for harming others with eruptions of their personal power when they enter a state of emotional disequilibrium such as anger. When we speak of someone "radiating hostility," it is almost a latent expression of the shamanic view.

A shaman would say that it is dangerous not to know about shamanism. In ignorance of shamanic principles, people do not know how to shield themselves from hostile energy intrusions through having guardian spirit power. Nor do they know that they, in turn, may be harming others unintentionally. Shamans believe that, because people are unaware that their hostile energies can penetrate others, they are unconsciously causing damage to their fellow human beings much of the time.

The shamanic removal of harmful power intrusions is difficult work, for the shaman sucks them out of a patient physically as well as mentally and emotionally. This technique is widely used in shamanic cultures in such distant areas as Australia, North and South America, and Siberia.

If you ever viewed the film *Sucking Doctor,* which shows the healing work of the famous California Indian shaman Essie Parrish, you saw a shaman pulling out intrusive power.[3] But Western skeptics say that the shaman is just pretending to suck something out of the person, an object that the shaman had already secreted in his mouth. Such skeptics have apparently not taken up shamanism themselves to discover what is happening.

What is happening goes back to the fact that the shaman is aware of two realities. As among the Jívaro, the shaman is pulling out an intrusive power that (in the SSC) has the appearance of a particular creature, such as a spider, and which he also knows is the hidden nature of a particular plant. When a shaman sucks out that power, he captures its spiritual essence in a portion of the same kind of plant that is its ordinary material home. That plant piece is, in other words, a power object. For example, the shaman may store in his mouth two half-inch-long twigs of the plant that he knows is the material "home" of the dangerous power being sucked out. He captures the power in one of those pieces, while using the other one to help. The fact that the shaman may then bring out the plant power object from his mouth and show it to a patient and audience as OSC evidence does not negate the nonordinary reality of what is going on for him in the SSC.

In the following adaptation of the sucking technique, the shaman does not store nor use pieces of plants in his mouth. This is because I have found that this particular use of material power objects seems to hinder, rather than help, Westerners in their shamanic sucking work. Odd as it may seem, Westerners often are at least as accepting of the intangibility of power as their primitive counterparts. Perhaps this is partly a result of the Westerners' knowledge of the invisibility of electrical energy and radiation. In any case, in this type of work the Western shaman appears to be most effective using only the SSC, or spirit, aspect of his plant helpers.

To accomplish sucking work successfully, the shaman must alert and marshal his spirit helpers to help him in the extraction of power intrusions from a patient. For this, the shaman uses one of his power songs. We have discussed these earlier, and in Chapter 5 I gave you the words to one that can also be used for this kind of work. Here are the words of another one, from a shaman of the Samoyed people of Siberia, for calling his spirits to work:

Come, come,
Spirits of magic,
If ye come not,
I shall go to you.
Awake, awake,
Spirits of magic,
I am come to you,
Arise from sleep.[4]

The procedure for extracting or removing a power intrusion is the same as undertaking the journey for a patient, up to a point. That point is usually very early in the journey before the shaman has gotten very far away from the entrance into the earth and while he is still in the Tunnel to the Lowerworld. If the patient has a harmful power intrusion, the shaman suddenly sees one of the following: voracious or dangerous insects, fanged serpents, or other reptiles and fish with visible fangs or teeth. He immediately stops the journey to deal with these intrusive powers. That is, the simple sight of one of these powers in the Tunnel is a signal that it should be removed immediately by sucking. *This work, however, should only be undertaken by a shaman who possesses two spirit helpers identical to the spirit of the power intrusion he has just seen.* If a shaman is not ready for this work, he either returns from the Tunnel or passes by the intrusive power spirit and proceeds to get a guardian spirit for the ill patient, which is essentially supportive treatment, until extraction of the intrusion can be done.

It is hard to explain, but the sight of one of these creatures in the Tunnel involves a complete certainty by the shaman that it is eating away or destroying a portion of the patient's body. At that moment, one may experience an incredible revulsion and an awareness that the insect or other creature is evil and the enemy of the shaman as well as of the patient. Even a Sioux medicine man such as Lame Deer, with great reverence for the plants and animals, shows this awareness when he says that the spider "has a power, too, but it is evil."[5] (See Plate 13.)

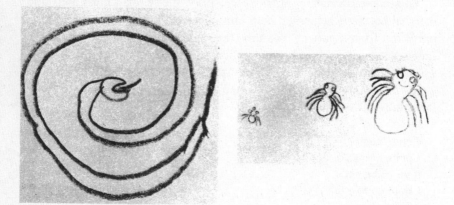

Plate 13.   Harmful intrusive powers in the form of spiders and a snake. Seen in patients' bodies by a Jívaro shaman while in the SSC. Drawn by him subsequent to the experiences.

This seeing, and passing by, of voracious or dangerous insects or other creatures is conveyed by Cloutier's poetic rendition of a Tsimshian shaman's healing journey experience:

Far away
huge bee-hives
I walk around
huge bee-hives

118

Spirit Bee
sees me
flies up high
shoots me

I'm bleeding all over
many arrows all over
I'm going to die
I'm going to die

far away
huge bee-hives
I walk around
huge bee-hives

Grandmother
sees me
her small boy
she heals me

she makes me grow
feeds me
small boy
inside

far away
huge bee-hives
I walk around
huge bee-hives[6]

If a qualified sucking shaman encounters the listed creatures in the Tunnel, and if he possesses two spirit helpers of the type he has just seen, he must immediately stop his journey and raise himself up from a lying position onto his knees. If the spirit canoe journeying method is being used, the drummer, on seeing the shaman get up, knows that the journey has been aborted, and immediately stops the drumming, leaving the canoe "dead in the water." The cessation of the drumming is also a message to all the crew members to stop their poling or paddling, since the journey has been stopped.

Remaining on his knees, the shaman starts to sing his power song, calling his spirit helpers to aid him in the sucking he is about to undertake. He also pulls toward him a basket or bowl containing sand or water, usually a container that he has used many times, in which to spit that which he extracts from the patient. Shaking the rattle over the

119

patient and singing powerfully, the shaman concentrates upon calling up his spirit helpers to aid him in the sucking (see Plate 14). The audience or crew members, now sitting in a circle facing in toward the patient and the shaman, contribute to this effort by joining in singing the power song.

The shaman must locate the harmful, intrusive powers within the patient. To this end he uses a divinatory technique. In the absence of taking *ayahuasca* to see into the patient, the shaman may use a technique that is something like employing a divining rod. In the SSC, with his eyes closed, he stretches out his free hand back and forth over the patient's head and body, slowly discovering if there is any special sensation of heat, energy, or vibration coming from any localized point in the patient's body. By passing his hand a few inches above the body slowly back and forth, an experienced shaman gets a definite sensation in his hand when it is over the place where the intrusive power lies. Another technique is to pass a feather over the patient to pick up any vibration.

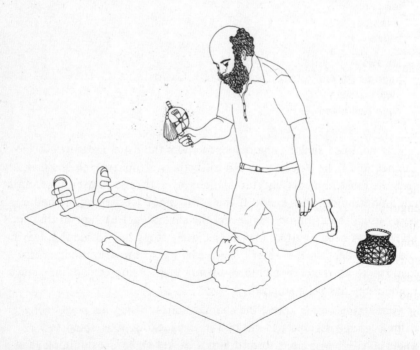

Plate 14.   *Preparing to suck out a harmful power intrusion. Drawn by Barbara Olsen.*

When the shaman senses the particular location, he calls the two spirit helpers, either silently or in song, as he shakes his rattle steadily over the patient. When he clearly sees the helpers approaching in the darkness, with his eyes still closed he wills them into his mouth. There they will capture and absorb the power intrusion as he sucks it out of the patient. When he definitely *sees* the two in his mouth, he wills all his other spirit helpers to assist him in the sucking. Now he is ready to begin the work of extraction.

At the location in the patient's body where he sensed the harmful intrusion, the shaman sucks with all his might (see Plate 15a). This can be done through clothing, but it is usually more efficacious to pull open the clothing at that spot and physically suck the skin where the intrusive power is located. This is an act involving not only the shaman's body, but his mind and emotions, which in the SSC are powerfully aroused and totally committed to the task.

The shaman has to be very careful in this process not to permit the voracious creature he saw from passing through his mouth and throat into his stomach. The creature is so emotionally repellent, however, that there is little likelihood of the shaman swallowing it. If by any chance he does, he should immediately seek the help of another sucking shaman in extracting it. (This is another reason why it is desirable for shamans to have partners.)

The shaman repeatedly sucks and "dry-vomits" as many times as necessary. *It is important not to swallow the sucked-out power, but to expel it after each sucking into the container on the floor or ground* (see Plate 15b). This is done with powerful, sometimes involuntary, violent retching that gives the shaman a real sense of cleansing, of being emptied of the emotionally disgusting power that he has extracted. As he removes the power intrusion from the patient, the shaman may feel engulfed in waves of extracted power that almost stun him and cause his body to tremble. After each time that he dry-vomits, he recovers his concentration by singing his power song and focusing on raising his spirit helpers again until he is strong enough to repeat the process. He keeps up such cycles of sucking until finally, in passing his hand back and forth above the patient, he no longer feels any localized emanations of heat, energy, or vibration.

Then he may continue to do some additional sucking at the places where he has already worked, or where he senses some residual dirtiness from the intrusive power, dry-vomiting into the container. When he no longer can sense any additional location of contamination or dirtiness,

121

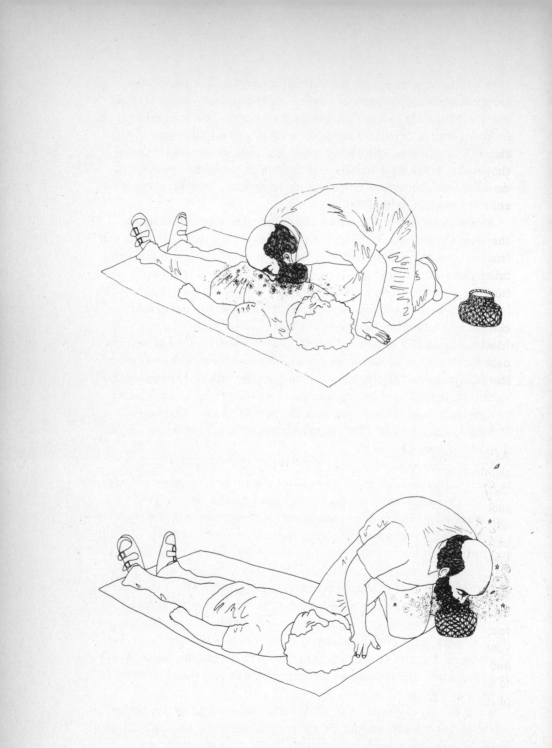

Plate 15. (a) Sucking out a power intrusion. (b) Expelling the power intrusion. Drawn by Barbara Olsen.

122

then he stops the sucking process. He may still sing his power song a bit longer to maintain the protective power of his animal and his spirit helpers around him.

Finally, when he is convinced the patient is spiritually clean, he shakes his rattle around the patient's body in a circular fashion four times to provide a definition of the unity of the cleansed area, demarcating its boundaries for the spiritual world. The patient then can either remain lying down or can sit up.

At this point it is important for the shaman to take the container of the vomited or expelled intrusive power out-of-doors and safely away from the patient and the group. There he throws away the contents. He brings back the container to refill it later with clean sand or water for further use when necessary.

Depending on the shaman's sense of power and his opinion of what is best to do, the journey can be begun over again immediately or delayed. Ideally, it is better for the journey to resume immediately so that the patient can now receive a power animal and thus be power-filled and therefore resistant to any additional harmful intrusions.

An Example

As I have indicated, one should undertake the sucking type of shamanism only if fully prepared, as set forth above. Yet in the case that follows, a beginning shaman with only slight knowledge of the sucking method found himself knowing what to do as the experience unfolded. This is not surprising, because once an apt student grasps the basic principles of shamanic power and healing, he can usually operate logically from those principles to solve new problems creatively. His description illustrates how the shaman casually moves back and forth between the SSC and the OSC in accomplishing a healing. The student decided to undertake the journey, which he thought would only be to recover a power animal, because of his deep concern for his friend, "a young woman in Vienna, who was much in conflict with her parents and was in a miserable state that day." He was not trained or prepared to suck out intrusive creatures, but he spontaneously did a creative job of removing the "dirtiness" just mentioned.

> Down I went as usual, but immediately after the entrance there was a left turn and suddenly all went black. None of the features I had earlier encountered, just black. To the right, just before the blackness, there was

123

an incredibly disgusting kind of slimy laocoon-mass, intertwined snakes, and spiders whose legs were black, blue, and red in color. After trying to go into the blackness on the left—which didn't work—I faced the mass to examine what I could do there. It was about two meters high—relative to me. It wouldn't go away, so after a while I started climbing up it—a filthy job, believe me! Overhead there was a chimney-like tube with rungs on one side, so I just went on climbing. The tube was vertical and dark at first, but got brighter as I went up. After climbing for a while, I still couldn't see an end, so I just let go of the rungs and flew the rest of the way. The tube was very high, and very bright at the top. I emerged into a sunlit landscape and found myself on the top of a flat roof.

I examined the roof. There was an entrance to a staircase that formed a triangular construction, sloping on one side with the door on the other. I climbed up the slope to peek inside from above. Just as I bent down to look I was grabbed by a bear and dragged inside. Down we went. The bear held me under his arm and just kept going. After a moment of apprehension I decided to wriggle myself out of his grip. I did. He never noticed and went his way. I then found myself in a long cavern, fairly bright and oval, which I later identified as the inside of my own torso. To my left [the side on which his patient was lying in ordinary reality] I noticed some cracks in the otherwise solid wall of the cavern. Black slime oozed out of some of the cracks. I pulled out some stones and more black slime poured out. Finally I got an opening big enough for me to go through, and I went in.

I found myself in a cave similar to the first one, only this one was filled knee-deep (in some places deeper) with this black slime. Towards the lower end there was an opening almost completely obstructed by black rocks and the slime that had built up there. I was wading knee-deep. Through the opening I could see light, like a warm sun, which was mostly hidden by the obstructions there. At first I didn't know what to do. So I got up on my knees [in ordinary reality] and started examining the patient's body from the outside with my hands. I could not get a clear sensation at first. It felt like it was covered with spider webs. I brushed them off with my fingers and then clearly felt a focus of energy—neither hot nor cold, yet both—around the stomach/ovary/bladder area. I sucked out what I could and got rid of it down the wash basin. It was very disgusting. After rinsing my mouth clean of any trace of whatever it was, I returned to my lying position next to the patient and went back into the cavern. The level of the black stuff was much lower now and it seemed a bit dryer too. I stood and looked around for a while not knowing what to do next.

Then I had an inspiration. I pulled off my pullover and lit it. With this torch I set fire to the slime everywhere in the cave. After a while it burned down to a substance that seemed like charcoal and black ashes. It was not slimy anymore. I don't know how I survived in there while everything was burning, but it didn't seem to be a problem. When the fire had stopped I examined the cavern some more and found—at the upper end—a tunnel leading away horizontally, large enough for a man to crawl through comfortably. In I went. After what seemed about five or six meters it dropped abruptly for about one or two meters and then bent back towards the direction of the cavern. I went in and found that it ended after two meters, widening slightly. I started digging in the floor at the end of the tunnel. Soon water started flowing up. I enlarged the hole and quickly left the tunnel as the water flowed stronger and threatened to inundate me.

The water flowed into the cavern with great force and washed the debris left by the fire towards the lower end of the cavern where the warm light could be seen dimly through a little hole. I went down there as the water pressure built up behind the rocks that obstructed the opening. I kicked at them a few times. The opening got larger and finally it was wide open. There was indeed a warm sun there. The filthy water poured towards it and was seen no more. Light and air began flooding the cavern from that end. It was not so dark anymore. I had done a good cleaning-up job, I realized. The cave walls and floor had a light color except for very few places where there were bits of black stuff left. The water formed into a brook running along the center of the cave to the lower end where it disappeared towards the sun that shone outside. (A very big sun! And quite close too!) With the fresh air that blew in from that end there came swallows. They flew around in the cavern, making it feel quite lively again. I took one with me when I came back from the cave and gave it [a power animal] to the patient.

At crucial points of my journey the patient started breathing heavily as if she could feel what was going on. She later explained she had been feeling a gradual loosening in her abdominal area. When I told her what I had found, she confirmed that she had digestive and ovary problems. In a letter six weeks later she reported changes for the better. The feeling of being stuck had gone and concrete conflicts were coming out into the open. I hope to see her again soon. Maybe we can establish a connection to the upper part of her body this time.

That's the story. Maybe you can use it in some way. I found it particularly interesting since I was so often at a loss about what to do, and yet ended up doing a lot of things no one had ever told me about.

One of the most famous North American Indian shamans to use the sucking method in recent decades was the late Essie Parrish. She was not just a see-er of power intrusions, but could hear them as well. She stated that when she was in trance, ". . . you can hear something in the patient laying there . . . you can hear the disease making noise. The disease in people's body is something like madness and they [the diseases] are living, lots of times they make noise, just like insects . . . they're living there like insects. . . ."[7]

Patients, both Indian and non-Indian, came long distances to be healed by Essie Parrish, and she often traveled to Nevada and Oregon in response to requests from the sick. She had received a vision that she should reveal her shamanic methods to non-Indian as well as Indian, so that everyone could eventually benefit from the knowledge. Because of that vision, she cooperated in making the *Sucking Doctor* film previously mentioned, and also explained her work to the spectators after her healing sessions. Since she was a specialist in extracting power intrusions, you may find the following account, recorded by Robert L. Oswalt, a valuable supplementary explanation of the sucking method of removing power instrusions.

The Work of a Sucking Doctor
Told by Essie Parrish

I am going to tell about treating people, since you want to know these things about me. I have been a doctor and will be one for all my life on this earth—that's what I was created for. I was put here on earth to cure people.

When I was young I didn't know about it—whenever I dreamed things (had visions)—because that was the only way that I dreamed.* I thought everyone was like that; I thought all children were that way. Those are the things that I used to tell about—things that I knew and saw.

The *first* person I cured was when I was more than twelve years old. At that time white doctors were hard to find; we were far away from any [white] medicine doctor.

One time my younger sister fell sick. She was so extremely sick with sores in her mouth that they thought she would die. My great-uncle, the one who raised her, must have been making plans when I didn't know about it—I was playing around outside. Unexpectedly they summoned me

---

* As Spott and Kroeber have pointed out with regard to shamanism among the Yurok of northern California, it is often difficult to distinguish in native accounts between dream or trance experiences (Spott and Kroeber 1942: 155). Often shamans and other primitive visionaries tend to group these two states of consciousness together in opposition to ordinary waking consciousness.

126

from inside the house. I still remember that; that was towards four o'clock in the evening.

Then when they had called me into the house he said, "Couldn't you do something for your little sister? I say to you that you possess a prophet's body.* You with your prophet's body could perhaps cure her. Couldn't you do something."

"I wonder what I should do now," I was thinking to myself because I was little and didn't know. But I said, "All right." That had been said to me. My power had told me, "If anyone ever asks anything of you, you should not say, 'No'; you are not for that purpose. You are one who fixes people. You are one who cures people." That's why I said, "All right."

After I had agreed, I prayed to heaven. My right hand I put on her head. When I had done so, a song that I didn't know came down into me. Amazingly that song came up out of me. But I didn't sing it out loud; it was singing down inside of me. "I wonder how I am going to cure her," I was thinking to myself. To my amazement she got well a few days afterward. That was the first person I cured. . . .

Unexpectedly another person got sick. They say he was about to die with what the white people call "double pneumonia." He was lying almost gone. It was a long way to a [white] medicine doctor. His older sister had come for me. She said, "I have come to ask you a great favor. I want you to see him. See him! Even though I see that he is dying, I want you to look at him."

Then when I had gone there I laid my hand on him here and there. And I sucked him. Amazingly it cured him. While I am doctoring I get better and better. Like the white people learn, I learn. Every time I treat people I move upward (in skill).

After a long time—several years—it was probably twelve or thirteen years—I moved still higher. Then I noticed that I had something in my throat to suck pains out with. And my hand power, I found out about my hand power. That power is always near me. But other people can't see it; I alone can see it.

When I sit there alongside a person, I call on Our Father.** That's my power—the one I call Our Father. Then it descends, my power comes down into me. And when that sick man is lying there, I usually see it (the power). These things seem unbelievable but I, myself, I know, because it is in me. I know what I see. *My* power is like that. You may doubt it if you don't want to believe; you don't have to believe but it is my work.

Way inside of the sick person lying there, there is something. It is just

* Mrs. Parrish was a prophet as well as a shaman.
** Mrs. Parrish was at one point the leader of the local Church of the Latter Day Saints and, as a master shaman, integrated some Christian concepts into her shamanism.

like seeing through something—if you put tissue over something, you could see through it. That is just the way I see it inside. I see what happens there and can feel it with my hand—my middle finger is the one with the power.

When I work with the hand power it is just like when you cast for fish and the fish tug on your bait—it feels like it would with the fish pulling on your line—that's what it is like. The pain sitting somewhere inside the person feels like it is pulling your hand towards itself—you can't miss it. It lets you touch it. I don't place my hand myself; it feels like someone— the disease—is pulling with a string. It is like what the white men call a 'magnet.' That's the way the disease in a person is—like a magnet.

And then it touches it. And when the power touches the pain, your breath is caught—it gets so that you can't breathe. But there is no fear. It is as if your chest were paralyzed—your breath is shut off. If you should breathe while holding that pain, the disease could hide itself. As the pain quiets your breathing, you can feel that pain there, with the result that your hand can take it out. However, if the breathing were not shut off I couldn't lift out the pain.

When I take it out you can't see it. You can't see it with your bare eyes, but I see it. Whenever I send it away, I see what the disease is. When the disease comes down into a person, which the white people talk about way differently; and we Indians too, we shamans, explain it way differently. That disease that comes down into a person is dirty; I suppose that is what the white people call "germs" but we Indian doctors call it "dirty."

I am going to talk about my hand power some more. The palm of the hand has power, and the finger in the middle of hand has power. That doesn't work just any time, only when I summon (power).

When there is a sick person somewhere to be found out, the hand power can find it out. Whenever someone thinks about it from somewhere, thinks toward me, there, on the tip of [the] middle finger, it acts as if shot—what the white people call "shock." If you touch something like electricity, you will know what the shock is like; that's how it acts there on the middle finger. When they think from somewhere, it is then that the power finds out, that it gives a warning. That is when I know that someone wants me. And it always turns out to be true. That is my hand power.

There is still a lot more to that (subject of doctoring). There is a doctoring power in my throat. Here, somewhere in the throat, the power sits. When that doctoring power first came down into me, I had already had some kind of growth there for about four years. It had affected me like diphtheria. I had almost died from its constricting (the throat) from the beginning, but I knew all along that it was becoming that (power).

128

But those that are staying with me didn't know; I had never told them about it. However, my power had told me saying, "That is because power has entered you there." When that happened (growth came), they called a white doctor to see me. The white doctor didn't recognize it; he told me that it was probably diphtheria. But I knew what it was. When that thing had finished growing there, I recovered.

That felt like a tongue lying there and it first moved when I sang. I was probably that way for four years with that thing lying there. After it grew on me, my voice improved. It told me for what purpose it was developing. It told me, "Power is developing." Without that I couldn't suck out any diseases. Only when it had developed could I suck out pains.

Then it gave me this staff with designs and said, "This is your power. Those designs on there are symbols. Those are disease words." And it spoke further saying, "There are many rules to this: You can't treat a menstruating woman and you can't doctor in a house where someone is menstruating. (In those situations) the power will not be your friend; the power will not rise for you." It has turned out to be true.

When I first doctored with my throat, it was for a young woman. When I treated her and sucked the disease out, something like a bubble came up out of my throat; just as it would if you blew up a big balloon, that is how it came from my mouth. Everyone there saw it. It had become inflated quite a lot when it floated from my mouth. Everyone saw it. Like foaming soap bubbles would look; that is how it looked at the start.

Ever since that happened I have been sucking diseases out. The disease that I suck out works like a magnet inside too (as when using hand power). On the place here where I said the power entered my throat, the disease acts as fast as electricity—it acts in [a] flash, like a magnet. And it shuts off the breath. When it does that, when it closes off the breath, like a magnet it comes along extremely slowly.

However, one doesn't notice how long he holds his breath. It's like being in what the white people call a "trance." While the disease is coming to me, I'm in a trance. It always speaks to me saying, "This is the way it is. It is such and such a kind of disease. This is why."

That disease flies and sticks to a certain place in the mouth. Our (shaman's) teeth have the power; there is something attached to our teeth. There is where the power is, on one certain tooth. There is where the disease sticks. Sometimes it flies under the tongue. When it sticks there it is extremely hard to release—it is, as I said, like a magnet. Then it dies there.

I spit out the dead disease. Then I let it fall into my hand so that many people can see it. They always see the disease that I suck out. But that is not to be touched by anyone else—it is contagious. Whoever picks the disease up, into him it would enter. Whenever it sits in my hand, it sticks

129

to it like a magnet. It won't fall off—even if you shake your hand it won't fall off. Even if you want to shake it loose it won't come loose.

You can put it in something like a piece of paper or a basket. If you are going to do that, you should sing for that purpose, you should call for that purpose. Some diseases sit for a while—sit for a few minutes—but others are fast. Some fast diseases stay just so many minutes after being put down and then disappear.

There is still much more (to tell about doctoring). In those many years that I have been treating people, I have seen many different kinds of disease.[8]

Tobacco Traps

Sucking out harmful power intrusions is, as we have seen, an advanced shamanic technique that requires considerable preparation. A much simpler technique involves what I call "tobacco traps," and is an adaptation of a method I learned from a Lakota Sioux medicine man in South Dakota. The method is based on the principle that the intrusive spirits enjoy tobacco, and are attracted to it. This is consistent with the Jívaro view, as you may recall, that the shaman keeps *tsentsak,* the spirits responsible for power intrusions, fed on tobacco water. This Sioux method involves the use of tobacco ties, or miniature cloth pouches containing tobacco.

In tobacco-trapping, the ties are used as bait to lure and catch intrusive spirits that may be within the body of a sick person. One of the ways in which this is done is to make a circle of tobacco ties around the patient, who is lying on the ground or the floor. Then when the shaman is working to remove harmful power intrusions from the patient, he also has the help of the tobacco ties in drawing the spirits out. When his extracting work is done, he carefully rolls up the tobacco ties in a ball and immediately takes them to a remote location. There the ball is unrolled and the tobacco ties draped over the branches of a tree, similar to the draping of tinsel on a Christmas tree. This is done to allow the spirits to disperse far from the humans whom they might harm.

An adaptation which I sometimes use is to employ the tobacco ties to cleanse an entire group of persons sitting together in a circle. In this approach, the string is held at one end of the circle by the person to the left of the shaman. The shaman then unrolls the string all the way around the circle in a clockwise direction, leaving adequate slack for

130

each person to tie on a tobacco tie. Next a large piece of red cloth is passed around the circle in the same direction, each person cutting out a small square with scissors, and passing the cloth and scissors on. A package of plain tobacco is passed, each person putting a pinch of tobacco (usually Bull Durham) into his small square of cloth, and folding the sides up to make a pouch. Then with concentration, each participant quietly takes his most serious individual pain and projects it into his tobacco pouch. Each person ties his tobacco pouch into the string. When everyone in the circle has done this, the shaman rises up and goes around the group on the outside of the circle, shaking his rattle. This is to help shake the pain, the hurt, the illness, the unhappiness, out of the individuals into their tobacco ties, which they hold before them. The shaman circles the group, shaking his rattle until he feels himself starting to enter the SSC.

When the shaman returns to his place and puts down his rattle, he now undertakes the most difficult part of the work. *To do this, he must be certain he is filled with power, so that none of the painful, illness-causing spirits that have been projected into the tobacco ties will be able to penetrate him.*

Singing his power song, he grasps one end of the string of tobacco ties and walks slowly into the center of the circle. He places that end carefully on the ground and keeps singing. Then slowly, and with great care, he starts pulling the string from the hands of the people in the circle, laying it down on the ground inside the circle into an ever-widening clockwise spiral. In the process the shaman may experience waves of despair, unhappiness, and pain washing over him as he slowly lays down the linked tobacco ties. He is sensing the pain that he is taking away from the people in the circle. It can be an almost overwhelming emotional experience. When finally the last end of the tobacco tie chain is on the ground, he continues to sing his power song to protect himself. He then, on his knees, slowly and carefully winds up the spiral into a ball, starting with the outer end. As he does this, he may feel an intense continuation of the feelings of pain, hurt, and unhappiness of the circle members.

As soon as the shaman is finished, he picks up the ball from the ground and carries it outstretched from him, walking rapidly away from the circle to a location at least a quarter of a mile away. There he unrolls the ball and drapes the ties onto a tree. He closes his eyes, pushes the power surrounding the tree away from him, and immediately

131

leaves. The others may watch him do this from a distance. Then they can all return together to their original location, sit together in a circle holding hands, and sing the power song.

Becoming the Patient

A related technique of shamanic healing is "becoming the patient." This method was taught to me by a Coast Salish Indian shaman in the State of Washington a few years ago. *As with other methods of removing harmful spirit intrusions, the shaman should practice this method only when he is power-full,* for in this technique he takes aboard or onto himself the power(s) causing harm to the patient. The invisible cloak of power surrounding the Coast Salish shaman prevents the spirits from intruding into him.[9]

The way one can use this approach is as follows. First the shaman discusses with the patient the nature of the pain or illness. He finds out everything he can about how the illness or pain feels, and develops a feeling for what it is like to be in this condition. He interrogates the patient as to the first onset of the affliction, learning about all the circumstances the patient was aware of at that time. Then he continues his questioning to learn what it is like to be the patient, what the patient's outlook on life is, what are the patient's problems and hopes. In other words, the shaman does his best to learn what it feels like to be the patient. This work, in contrast to psychoanalysis, normally only covers a few days, depending upon the skills of the shaman and his rapport with the patient.

When the shaman is satisfied that he can identify emotionally with the patient, he is ready to undertake the critical phase of the healing work.

At this point the shaman and the patient go to a wilderness location devoid of human habitation. The shaman, with his rattle and power song, wakes his guardian spirit to help him. The patient sits quietly beside him during this phase.

When the shaman feels power-full, he and the patient slowly take off their clothes and exchange them with each other. As the shaman puts on each article of the patient's clothing he concentrates on taking on the patient's hurts and afflictions and on assuming the patient's personality. By the time the shaman puts on the last piece of clothing, the shaman should now begin to feel that he *is* the patient.

Now the shaman and the patient start dancing, accompanied by the shaman's rattle. The shaman imitates every movement and gesture of the patient to become the patient. Then, when the shaman feels his consciousness changing, he holds his hands against the patient's body until he feels that he has taken on all that is necessary for the patient—and all that he feels he can safely carry—of the patient's affliction. If the work is done right, the shaman will feel waves of sickness, or pain, passing over him.

At that moment, the shaman runs away several hundred feet into the uninhabited wilderness, stops, and stretches out his arms before him. He focuses with all his strength upon "throwing away" the painful intrusive power that was causing harm to the patient and now is resting on him. With actual physical motions of his arms, and with whatever sounds that emerge, the shaman throws the harm-causing power into the distant sky, toward the horizon, with all his force.

This sending-away process may take several minutes or more. The shaman will know when he is finished by the sense of the removal from his body of the patient's affliction and of the patient's personality. The shaman will feel cleansed and relaxed.

He now returns to the patient and they re-exchange their clothing. The shaman finishes the work by singing a power song and standing together with the patient in the smoke of a fire containing wild sage or cedar boughs to complete the cleansing.

A modification of this technique, especially for demonstration purposes, may be used in groups at workshops. First the group goes to a wild area, uninhabited by humans. A volunteer sits in the center of the circle of participants and is interviewed for a brief period of time by the entire group. Each member asks one question regarding how the patient experiences the pain or illness, the conditions of the onset of illness, the likes and dislikes of the patient, and anything else that will help them learn to feel like that patient. In this exercise, it is not desirable for nonshaman participants individually to take on much of the power causing the harm to the patient. The procedure to be described thus permits all of them to take on only a small portion of the harmful intrusive power, so as not to jeopardize themselves. It is important for the leader of the group to tell any participants who do not feel power-full not to participate, but simply to be spectators.

Then the patient is asked to dance in any way he pleases. Members of the group shake rattles and beat a drum, continually adjusting their tempo to that of the dancer. Volunteers are asked to imitate in every possible way the dancing of the patient, by dancing alongside him.

Every movement of the patient should be mimicked.

When each of the dancers reaches the point where he feels emotionally that he has to some degree, become the patient, he should touch the patient only briefly, draw some of the intrusive power from him, and run away several hundred feet, face the wilderness, and throw the power away from him as earlier described.

When all the dancers have done this, and feel cleansed, they return to the group and embrace the patient. All join together to form a power circle by holding hands, incorporating the patient into it, and the group sings a power song (subsequently a journey can be undertaken to restore the power animal for the patient).

Obviously, this technique has an interesting resemblance to psychoanalysis, including the principle of countertransference, and is an illustration of how shamanic techniques often foreshadow aspects of healing methods developed only recently in the West. The "becoming the patient" method of the Coast Salish also has an analogue among the !Kung Bushmen of southern Africa, whose shamans:

> . . . place their fluttering hands on either side of the person's chest, or wherever the sickness is located. They touch the person lightly, or more often vibrate their hands close to the skin's surface. At times the healer wraps his body around the person, rubbing his sweat—believed to carry healing properties—on the sick person. The sickness is drawn into the healer. Then the healer expels the sickness from his own body, shaking it from his hand out into space, his body shuddering with pain.[10]

In the !Kung healing, the shaman "pulls out the sickness with eerie, earth-shattering screams and howls that show the pain and difficulty of his healing." The work lasts several hours.[11]

Afterword

Albert Schweitzer reportedly once observed, "The witch doctor succeeds for the same reason all the rest of us [doctors] succeed. Each patient carries his own doctor inside him. They come to us not knowing this truth. We are at our best when we give the doctor who resides within each patient a chance to go to work."[1]

Perhaps the shaman is uniquely qualified among the practitioners of the healing arts to give "the doctor inside a chance to go to work." While the lack of modern medical technology may have forced primitive peoples to develop their latent shamanic powers for healing, even today it is increasingly recognized that "physical" health and healing sometimes require more than technological treatment. There is a new awareness that "physical" and "mental" health are closely connected, and that emotional factors can play an important role in the onset, progress, and cure of illness. The recent accumulation of experimental evidence that yogic practitioners and biofeedback subjects can manipulate basic body processes previously thought by Western medicine to be uncontrollable by the mind is only part of the new recognition of the relevance of spiritual and mental practices to health. Particularly exciting, and implicitly supportive of the shamanic approach to health and healing, is the new medical evidence that in an altered state of consciousness the mind may be able to will the body's immune system into action through the hypothalamus. Possibly science will eventually find that the unconscious mind of the shaman's patient, under the influence of sonic driving, is being "programmed" by the ritual to activate the body's immune system against disease.

The burgeoning field of holistic medicine shows a tremendous amount of experimentation involving the reinvention of many techniques long practiced in shamanism, such as visualization, altered state of consciousness, aspects of psychoanalysis, hypnotherapy, meditation, positive attitude, stress-reduction, and mental and emotional expression of personal will for health and healing. In a sense, shamanism is being reinvented in the West precisely because it is needed.

Connected with a growing realization of the inadequacies of purely technological treatment of illness is a dissatisfaction with the impersonality of modern commercial and institutional medicine. In the primitive world, shamans are frequently members of the same extended family as the patient, with an emotional commitment to the personal well-being of the patient not typical of the fifteen-minute doctor's office visit of contemporary society. The shaman may work all night, or several nights, for the recovery of a single patient, involving himself and the patient in a dyadic alliance that intertwines the unconscious of both in a heroic partnership against disease and death. But the alliance is more, for it is an alliance with the hidden powers of Nature, unseen in daylight where the material impingements of daily life clutter consciousness. Instead, the pair, the shaman and patient together, venture into the clarity of darkness, where uninterrupted by external and superficial stimuli, the shaman *sees* the hidden forces involved with the depths of the unconscious, and harnesses them or combats them for the welfare and survival of the patient. Some shamans, of course, are not members of the patients' families, and indeed in some societies accept payment for their work. But, as among the Tsimshian Gitksan of the Northwest Coast of North America, it is not uncommon for the shaman to return payment if the patient dies.[2]

The achievements of Western scientific and technological medicine are, of course, miraculous in their own right. But I hope that eventually shamanic knowledge and methods will be respected by Westerners, just as shamans respect Western technological medicine. With mutual respect, both strategies can help realize the holistic approach to healing and health that so many people are seeking. To use shamanism, we do not need to understand in scientific terms why it works, just as we do not need to know why acupuncture works in order to benefit from it.

There is no conflict between shamanic practice and modern medical treatment. Every North or South American Indian shaman I have ever asked about this matter has agreed there is no competition whatsoever. Jívaro shamans are perfectly willing to have their patients go see a missionary doctor, for example. In fact, they encourage their patients to get all the technological treatment possible. The shaman wants, first and foremost, to see the patient well. Any kind of technological treatment or medication that will contribute to the strength of the patient, that will help combat any kind of illness, is welcome.

A current example of a mutually supportive combination of shamanism with Western technological medicine is the well-known work of Dr. O. Carl Simonton and Stephanie Matthews-Simonton in treating cancer patients. Although the Simontons did not knowingly pursue shamanic methods, some of their techniques in support of chemotherapy are incredibly similar to those of shamans. The Simontons' patients are reportedly sometimes surprisingly successful in gaining relief from pain and in achieving the remission of their cancerous conditions.[3]

As part of their treatment, patients relax in a quiet room and visualize themselves on a walking journey until they meet an "inner guide," which is a person or an animal. The patient then asks the "guide" for help in getting well.[4] This resemblance to the shamanic journey, the recovery of a power animal, and its shamanic use is as obvious as it is remarkable.

Furthermore, the Simontons, without suggesting the content, had their patients visualize and make drawings of their cancers.[5] The patients spontaneously drew snakes and other creatures surprisingly similar to those seen by shamans as harmful intrusive powers in the bodies of their patients. (See, for example, the Jívaro drawings in Plate 13.) The Simontons now encourage their patients to visualize their cancers as "pain creatures" and to get rid of them.[6]

But the similarity to shamanism does not stop there. The Simontons found that they could train their patients to visualize the sending of their white blood cells to ingest the cancerous cells and expel them from the body much as a shaman visualizes and commands his spirit helpers to suck up and remove harmful power intrusions from the body of his patient. One of the main differences is that the Simontons' patients are acting as their own healers, something that is difficult for even the best of shamans. Perhaps the cancer patients might be further helped by

137

having a shaman work with them. A patient should not be required to be his own shaman any more than he should be required to limit his technological treatments to the self-administration of patent medicines purchased from the local drugstore.

One day, and I hope it will be soon, a modern version of the shaman will work side-by-side with orthodox Western physicians. In fact, this is already starting to take place where native shamans exist, as on some North American Indian reservations and in some places in Australia. Equally exciting is the prospect of physicians being trained in shamanic methods of healing and health maintenance so they can combine both approaches in their practice. I am happy to note that small numbers of younger physicians have already participated in my training workshops and seem enthusiastic about what they have learned. Only time will tell how successful they are in implementing shamanic principles in their work.

Whatever your own interests and hopes with regard to the way of the shaman, a basic question exists: Where do you go from here? You do not have to become a shaman in order to continue the work described in this book. Being a shaman entails seriously trying to help people who have problems of power and health. You may not feel comfortable taking such a responsibility. Even in primitive societies most people do not. But you can still work to help yourself by seriously and regularly using the methods you have learned here. You can work alone, even without a drummer, by using the cassette recording of shamanic drumming referred to in Appendix A. Thus is twentieth century technology combined with shamanism!

For those of you who wish to become professional shamans, I must point out that there is more to experience and learn than is dealt with in the preceding pages, such as: wilderness wandering, the vision quest, the shamanic experience of death and resurrection, the Orphic journey, shamanism and afterlife, journeying to the Upperworld. Meanwhile, however, the most important thing is for you to practice regularly what you have learned. You can be assisted in this by a friend or relative willing to work with you as a partner, by participating in shamanic training workshops, and by developing a circle of shamanically inclined persons who meet regularly to help one another and others.

As I have noted, you can work simply to help yourself, but you may not find that sufficient and wish to help others shamanically. Your biggest obstacles in this will be cultural and social, not shamanic, for we live in the very civilization that persecuted and destroyed those who possessed the ancient knowledge. You will not be burned at the stake, but you will not receive the Nobel Prize in medicine, either.

Among the Koryak of Siberia there was a useful distinction between family shamanism and professional shamanism.[7] Family shamanism was the helping of immediate relatives by those who were less advanced or less powerful in shamanic knowledge. Professional shamanism was practiced by those more advanced and powerful, and involved the treatment of any and all clients. If you wish to help others shamanically, I suggest you follow the family shamanism model, working to help close friends and family members who are sympathetic. And remember, work to *supplement* orthodox Western medical treatment, not to compete with it. The objective is not to be a purist, but to help others achieve health and happiness, and harmony with Nature, in every practical way.

In shamanism there is ultimately no distinction between helping others and helping yourself. By helping others shamanically, one becomes more powerful, self-fulfilled, and joyous. Shamanism goes far beyond a primarily self-concerned transcendence of ordinary reality. It is transcendence for a broader purpose, the helping of humankind. The enlightenment of shamanism is the ability to light up what others perceive as darkness, and thereby to *see* and to journey on behalf of a humanity that is perilously close to losing its spiritual connectedness with all its relatives, the plants and animals of this good Earth.

I leave you now with a poem by Josie Tamarin, one of the small but growing number of young people who are exploring the way of the shaman.[8] The poem serves to remind us that it is in the practice of shamanic methods we find the way no one else can find for us. As a spirit told a Siberian Samoyed shaman, "Shamanizing, you will find your way, by yourself."[9]

song for the journey

the eagle soars into turquoise and indigo
catching gold on white tipped feathers
in cadence of wind and stillnesses
singing and swooping with currents and storms
alone, the far-seer, sky dancer.
sun fire dips down to serpentine underworld
and eagle descends on rose and mauve and amber light
to an eyrie for night's long dream

head curved under wings
eagle encircled in sleep

reflecting early kinship
with those scaled and coiled beings
who swallow the sun in their tangled trap
while the lost world waits in darkness and dream;
and in dreamworlds gods and goddesses
beat the pulse of prayer
dancing near smaller fires
drumming toward greater light
creating song from cries of loss
fanning the glowing ember of the heart
praising color:
green of growth, gold of maize
soft rich browns of deer and earth
rainbow prisms of mist and sun
and riotous spring anemonies
tangerine and sienna of autumn's burnt lemon death
after summer's blue heat
and the white quiet in the center
of winter's stillness

and as hope begins to flicker
in the endless dark tunnel of night
eagle dreams stir
and in sleep awaken shadow-winged predator spirits
who dive for us all
into alien elements
fathomless seas of cobalt and black
dive through the surface
along watery crescents of moon's mirrored image
downward liquid spiral journey
and now is our need for eagle's sharp vision:
glimpse of turbulence below
dark shapes massing and twisting
in volcanic force the sun is caught
by serpents jealous and frenzied in battle
surrounding the light;
beak and talons curve
wings pull against the tidal vortex
moving with but not surrendering
to that power
and they strike

for an endless moment hearts stop in their sleep

drums do not beat
as feathers, coils, silver fangs and claws
embrace in the death of our dreams;
and in that moment the sun is freed
and begins to float luminous
toward that thin membrane where sea and sky meet
leaving an image of frozen fury far below
and finally, bursting through
with the fragile sound of silence and color
dawn is borne up on wings of light

life stirs
light stirs us all
and an eagle soars toward the sun
on the sighs of our awakening

APPENDIX A

Drums, Drumming Cassettes, and Training Workshops

At the time the first edition of this book appeared in 1980, it was difficult to find appropriate drums for shamanic work. One of the few types of suitable drums that could be easily obtained was the two-headed Taos Indian type from New Mexico, made from a hollowed-out cottonwood log and covered with rawhide. This is the kind shown in the preceding illustrations. Although heavy and cumbersome, it is the type I occasionally still use to obtain a deep tone.

Drums

Today drums suitable for shamanic work are much more readily available, including many excellent ones that resemble the classic shamanic drums of Siberia and the Northwest Coast of North America. These are lightweight, round frame drums with a single head, held in one hand. They are easy to support when standing, moving, or drumming for a long period of time, and often have more resonance indoors than the double-headed Taos drums. These are the ones I recommend for your use, and they are the ones I also mainly use myself. I suggest single-headed round frame drums that are 16″ to 17″ in diameter. They are large enough to provide adequate volume, but not so large as to be too heavy to support with one arm for an extended time.

Of these single-headed round frame drums, there are two basic kinds: (1) those with a synthetic, or mylar, head; and (2) those with a traditional rawhide or leather head. The mylar-covered single-headed round frame drum is relatively inexpensive, widely-available, and a good beginning drum. Also its head is relatively unaffected by changes in temperature and humidity, unlike skin-covered drums.

The mylar-headed drum is manufactured under the label, "REMO Pre-Tuned Hand Drum," and can be ordered through most musical instrument stores in North America. I recommend the 16″ one (#PTS 8516 HD). You will need to drill 4 to 6 holes in the frame and pass a leather thong or cord back and forth between the holes to create a "web" to grasp with one hand. This improves the resonance. As a beater, I suggest a tympani mallet, such as the "Sonor 8," also available through musical instrument stores.

As you become more experienced in shamanic work, you may wish to obtain a more expensive rawhide or leather-covered single-headed round frame drum. Unlike the mylar-headed type, this kind of drum should be protected from excessive heat, dryness, and extreme moisture. It is a good idea to consult the maker on the specific care of such a drum. Many craftspersons now construct them, and a list of them can be obtained from the Foundation for Shamanic Studies at the address given below.

If you enjoy working with your hands, you may eventually wish to make your own drum. To guide you in this, I highly recommend the paperback book, *How to Make Drums, Tomtoms and Rattles: Primitive Percussion Instruments for Modern Use* by Bernard S. Mason, published by Dover Publications, 180 Varick Street, New York, New York 10014.

Rattles

The Hopi, Zuni, and Rio Grande Puebloan peoples of the Southwestern United States make excellent, beautifully decorated rattles from dried gourds. These can usually be found for sale in Native American crafts stores in Santa Fe, New Mexico. An easier and less expensive way to get a rattle is through your local musical instrument store. I recommend the "Professional Maraca" (LP 281), manufactured by Latin Percussion. Although made of plastic and not particularly attractive, it is superior to the majority of commercially-sold maracas, having the strong, sharp sound of many tribal shaman's rattles.

If you wish to make a rattle, you can cut the narrow end off a gourd, put in very small pebbles, glass beads, or bird shot, and epoxy a wooden handle onto the gourd. The book by Mason, mentioned above, can provide you with additional advice. If you wish to grow your own, seeds for a wide variety of gourds are listed in the catalog of the Park Seed Company, Greenwood, South Carolina 20647.

Drumming Cassettes

Drumming cassettes, if specifically created for shamanic journeying, can provide excellent sonic support when properly used. A single side of a cassette, for example, can furnish half an hour of journeying time, a substantially longer period than live drumming usually lasts.

I first developed a drumming tape in 1979 to help readers of the 1980 edition of this book who lacked drums. However, I never expected the cassette to be as effective as a live drum. Then, in the early 1980s, while working with shamanic counseling clients using the tape, I discovered an improved way to journey with the drumming tape, a technique now called "simultaneous narration." In this method, the recumbent journeyer, with eyes covered in a darkened room, and playing the drumming tape through headphones, describes the journey aloud simultaneously as he or she experiences it. Surprisingly, the technique usually makes journeying easier and often at least twice as vivid as when the person simply remains silent.

A supplementary innovation is for the journeyer to wear a lapel microphone connected to a tape recorder (separate from the tape player providing the drumming through headphones) and to make a recording of the simultaneous narration. This not only provides the person with a permanent taped record of the journey experience, but also permits an immediate review and analysis of the experience and of the information gained. Workshops and courses providing training in this method are given by the Foundation for Shamanic Studies in its Shamanic Counseling Training programs (see below).

In my experience, using headphones to obtain this sonic driving input is generally more effective than employing a speaker system, and is less disturbing to housemates and neighbors. In addition, headphones are essential if the simultaneous narration technique is used, since the sound of speakers tends to drown out the recording of the narration.

The classic cassette for use with this book is *Drumming for the Shamanic Journey*, produced by the Foundation for Shamanic Studies and available from the Foundation or book stores carrying New Age music. The drumming cassette should be used with stereo cassette players having the Dolby noise reduction system to reduce hiss, which can be distracting when journeying. The Foundation cassettes have the callback signal, described for live drumming in this book, at the end of the approximately one-half hour that constitutes one side. If only a fifteen-minute journey is desired, simply start the tape midway in order to get the callback signal.

The Foundation also has available high-quality compact discs and shamanic journey drumming.

Shamanic Training Workshops and Programs

If you wish to obtain first-hand training in shamanism and shamanic healing, a schedule of workshops and training programs given by me and my associates at various locations in the United States and elsewhere is available from:

The Foundation for Shamanic Studies
P.O. Box 1939
Mill Valley, California 94942
Telephone: (415) 380-8282

This non-profit organization also supports—with the income from workshops, memberships, and donations—programs to preserve, transmit, and apply shamanic knowledge to contemporary problems of the Planet. These programs include Urgent Tribal Assistance (UTA), Shamanism and Health (SAH), and Shamanism for Healing the Earth (SHE).

The Hand Game of the Flathead Indians

as described by Alan P. Merriam[1]

This excellent description of the rules and methods of the Flathead hand game was based upon fieldwork conducted by Merriam in Montana in the summer of 1950. The rules and practices are relatively similar to those played today by Salish and other tribes in the Northwest. There is also a recording of Flathead *Stick Game Songs* that can help you understand how it is played.[2]

The preliminaries to the game are informal, beginning with any individual who has the desire and enthusiasm to start a game. It is he who sets up the physical requirements for the game, which consist of two poles or boards of any convenient size and weight and perhaps ten to fifteen feet in length. These boards or poles are laid on the ground about five feet apart and parallel to each other. . . . The first man on each side usually becomes the "captain" of his side, although this rule is not inviolable; in any case, if he can write, he ordinarily takes the bets for his side and writes the names and amounts wagered on a piece of paper.

When the bets have become sufficient, or more exactly, when no more seem to be forthcoming, the players, including anyone who has bet and wishes to play, take sticks, any piece of wood of a convenient length for striking a rhythm on the pole or board in front of him, and sit down behind the parallel boards, the two sides thus facing each other. In general, the number of players on each side is eight to ten; the game may be played with as many players as desired, although one seldom sees more than a dozen or fewer than five players on each side.

The captain has charge of five wooden pegs, each about eight to ten inches long, sharpened at one end, and about three-quarters of an inch in diameter. These sticks are usually painted in bright colors and thus can be easily identified by the onlooker.

At the time the author was watching the stick game two sets of sticks seemed to be in most general use. In one of these all ten sticks were painted a light blue, and in the other all were painted in alternating red and yellow bands; in the latter case the alternations were reversed for the two sets of five sticks each, that is, in one case red and yellow, and in the other yellow and red. These five sticks on each side are stuck in the ground in front of the parallel poles, usually leaning away from the players.

Once the sticks have been settled, two sets of two bones each are displayed. These bones vary in size and to a certain extent in shape, depending upon whether they are men's or women's bones. Men's bones, that is, bones which are used by men, are in general taken from the leg bone of a horse; they are approximately two and five-eighths inches long and an inch in diameter. The bones are highly polished and, in the instance of the most popular set used at the time of observation, were given a coating of light blue paint at the ends in a strip approximately a quarter of an inch wide. This particular set of men's bones was part of a matching set of gambling equipment with the blue counting sticks referred to above; they were owned by one of the most persistent stick game gamblers on the reservation. While the marked bone was formerly distinguished by bands of sinew or rawhide wrapped around the middle, the most common marking at present takes the form of three bands of black electrician's tape each three-eighths of an inch wide and separated by an open space of about one-eighth inch.

Women's bones, on the other hand, are considerably smaller, in deference, it is explained, to the fact that women's hands are smaller than men's. Often made from the leg bone of a deer, they are usually about two and a quarter inches long and three-quarters to seven-eighths of an inch in diameter. The marked bone is again distinguished by black electrician's tape, but usually with only two bands instead of three. . . .

There are at least two ways in which the game may be started, the first of which is perhaps more "proper" than the second. The "captain" of each side takes a pair of bones, that is, one marked and one unmarked bone, hides them in his fists in a manner to be described below, and once hidden, extends his fists in front of him and to the sides. Each "captain" then guesses the position of the unmarked bone held by

147

the other; if each guesses correctly, or if each guesses incorrectly, it is a standoff and the process is repeated. However, if one guesses correctly and the other incorrectly, the latter must give up his bones and one counting stick. Real play then begins. In the second possible starting play, one "captain," usually the one who has begun the preliminaries by laying down his bet first, takes one set of bones and hides them. Holding one in each closed fist, he challenges his opposite number to guess the positions; if the guesser is correct, the bones and one counting stick go to his side. If he is incorrect, the process is reversed. This second method of beginning the game, which gives at least a psychological advantage to the side which holds the bones, is seldom used.

As soon as the first position of the bones has been determined by one of the methods described above, the side which has gained possession bursts into song, at the same time beating on the parallel board or pole with the short sticks picked up before the game. The "captain" holds both pairs of bones, and after some singing and pantomime, he throws one set to a person, perhaps keeping the other set himself or perhaps passing them also to another person. Those who receive the bones immediately drop their sticks and begin the elaborate pantomime which accompanies the hiding process. The selection of those who are to hide the bones is apparently purely arbitrary, although those who can manipulate them best, or those who are known to be lucky in the stick game, are obviously most often chosen.

The pantomime which accompanies the game takes several forms, and the ability of a player is often judged by the skill with which he hides the bones. Informants often said, "You have to know the motions to be a good stick game player." At the same time, there seems to be no particular significance in any of the motions. The player is usually on his knees if a man, and sitting cross-legged if a woman. Men usually throw the bones in the air as a preliminary gesture, catch them, and bend over until the face is actually touching the ground, at this point hiding the bones behind the chest. One is then likely to straighten up again and show his opponents how he has held the bones, and repeat the process with variation. He may hold the bones behind his back, or quite characteristically, with his arms crossed and hands in the opposite armpits. Again, at the end of the preliminary motions, the final hiding often takes place under a hat or a handkerchief placed on the ground in front of the player. Women are most likely to manipulate the bones inside the shirtfront, under a shawl or handkerchief, or behind the back; they also often borrow a hat from a man under which the bones may be changed from hand to hand. One also frequently sees a woman holding a large handkerchief in her mouth, singing all the while, under which she hides the bones. During this preliminary play, the side with the bones is

148

constantly singing, shouting, and insulting the players on the opposing side. The bones are constantly hidden, exposed to the view of the opposing players, and re-hidden; the preliminary play may continue for a full ten minutes in extreme cases.

In the meantime, the side which is to make the guess is silent for the most part. The actual guesser is most often the "captain," although he may designate the responsibility to another person. . . . Characteristically, he points at one or the other of the players, using a particular gesture in which the left hand is brought sharply to the right shoulder, and as it hits the shoulder, the right arm extends from a position at which it is bent at the elbow. Thus it appears as though the striking by the left hand propels the right arm out straight. As the arm stretches out, the first finger only is extended, pointing toward one of the people who has the bones. This is then repeated to point at the other player, and may be repeated throughout the manipulation of the bones; such motions, however, do not constitute a real guess.

The two players with the bones work independently; when one is ready to accept a guess he signifies his intention by extending both arms away from his sides, the knuckles toward the guessers, thus hiding the bones in his clenched fists; the other player soon follows suit. In presenting the bones for guessing, one hand is sometimes extended while the other is crossed over the breast and concealed under the opposite armpit. The guess must be made rapidly or the bones will be withdrawn and the manipulation begun again. The guesser indicates his guess with the motion described above; in the case of a definite choice, the arm motion is accompanied by an audible grunt which signifies the final decision has been made. Four possible guesses may be made, all applying to both sets of bones: 1. if the guesser points to the right with the index finger, it indicates that he believes both unmarked bones are in his two opponents' left hands; 2. if he points to the left, he signifies his decision that the two unmarked bones are in the players' right hands; 3. if he points straight ahead with arm slanting toward the ground, he indicates his belief that the two unmarked bones are in the center; that is, in the right hand of the player to his right, and in the left hand of the player to his left; 4. if he extends the thumb and first finger, palm upward, with the other three fingers closed, he indicates his decision that the unmarked bones are on the outside; that is, in the left hand of the player to his right, and in the right hand of the player to his left.

Should the guesser make an incorrect guess on both bones, he must turn over two counting sticks to the opposing side; should he guess correctly on both, he receives both pairs of bones, but no sticks. If he guesses one set correctly, those bones are thrown over to him, but the other set is retained by the original side, and the guesser must give up

149

one stick. In other words, possession of the bones lasts as long as the guesser is fooled; a wrong guess costs him a stick. The game can thus be won when one side has possession of but one set of bones, since before play can be begun by a side, it must win possession of both sets. When possession of both sets of bones has been won, the second side begins singing, beating the board, and hiding the bones.

In order to complete a game, one side must win all ten sticks, although each side begins the game with five. As noted above, the sticks are placed in the ground leaning away from the players and in front of the parallel board before them. As sticks are won, they are placed behind the board until all ten have been put in play; in this position they are either stuck in the ground again or laid in a neat pile. Once all ten sticks have been placed behind the parallel poles, the game is fully under way. Thus supposing that side A is in possession of the bones at the start of the game, and A makes six straight wins; this, of course, means it has won more sticks than are possessed by side B. In this case, side B throws over its five sticks, but on the sixth successful win, side A will take one stick from in front of the board and place it behind the board, thus putting a sixth stick in play. If then side A loses the bones and then makes an incorrect guess, it must pay with a fresh stick, not a stick it has won from side B.

Play is continued, then, until one side has won all ten sticks. . . .

Empathy and a sort of "divination" play a part in the game. For example, when one side has but one stick left it is almost invariably stuck in front of the pole and pounded vigorously into the ground by the "captain"; this, of course, supposedly makes it harder for the other side to obtain possession. When one side has guessed and won one set of bones, those bones are thrown over immediately. Often the "captain" of the side will then manipulate them, although he, of course, must still obtain the other set; he may look at the bones in his hand, show them to the crowd and then make his guess according to the way his pair has fallen.

The stick game is played today by men only, women only, or mixed teams. Small children are encouraged to join in, and on many occasions the "captain" will throw the bones to children to hide, children so small that their fists barely cover the bones. On such an occasion, considerable encouragement is given the child.

Notes

See Bibliography for complete source information

Preface to the Third Edition

1. The original edition (Harner 1980) was published by Harper & Row; the second edition (Harner 1982) by Bantam Books.
2. For additional information on this movement, see Doore 1988, Drury 1989, Nicholson 1987, Townsend 1987, and the quarterly publications, *Foundation for Shamanic Studies Newsletter,* and *Shaman's Drum.*
3. E.g., see Achterberg 1985, Dossey 1988, Grof 1988, and Lawlis 1988.
4. Eliade 1964: 99.
5. For additional information on shamanic counseling, see Harner 1988.

Introduction

1. E.g., Mandell 1978; 73.
2. Elkin 1945: 66-67; 72-73.

Chapter 1: Discovering the Way.

1. Their names have been changed.
2. This narrative does not imply recommendation of *ayahuasca* or *maikua* use by the reader. Datura species, in fact, are quite toxic and their ingestion can produce serious untoward effects, including death.
3. Fuller accounts of Jívaro shamanism may be found in Harner 1972: 116-124, 152-166; and in Harner 1968 or 1973a.

Chapter 2: The Shamanic Journey: Introduction

1. Eliade 1964: 5.
2. Lowie 1952: *xvi-xvii.*

3. Rasmussen 1929: 112.
4. Ibid.: 118-119.
5. Eliade 1964: 138; Elkin 1945: 96-97; Howitt 1904; 406, 582-583.
6. Harner 1968: 28; Harner 1973a: 15-16.
7. Bogoras 1904-1909: 441.
8. Ibid.: 438.
9. Rasmussen 1929: 124.
10. Elkin 1945: 107, 108.
11. Halifax 1979: 56, after Biesele 1975.
12. Spencer and Gillen 1927: 424, 266.
13. Eells 1889: 667.
14. **Rasmussen 1929: 126.**
15. **Ibid.: 127.**
16. **Popov 1968: 138.**
17. **Essie Parrish of the Kashia Pomo, personal communication, 1965.**
18. **Boas 1900: 37.**
19. **Mc.Gregor 1941: 304-305.**
20. **Bunzel 1932: 528-534. Also Bunzel, personal communication, 1980.**
21. **Mc.Gregor 1941: 259-260.**
22. **E.g., Ibid.: 301-302.**
23. **Vastokas 1973/1974: 137.**

Chapter 3: Shamanism and States of Consciousness

1. Eliade 1964.
2. E.g., Halifax 1979: 3.
3. Furst 1972: *ix*.
4. Wilbert 1972: 81-82.
5. Benedict 1923: 67.
6. See Harner 1973c.
7. Devereux 1957: 1036.
8. See Harner 1972: 134-169; or 1973a.
9. Hultkrantz 1973: 31.
10. Stanner 1956: 161.
11. Hultkrantz 1973: 28, 31.
12. Eliade 1964: 222-223.
13. Hultkrantz 1973: 28.
14. Reinhard 1975: 20.
15. Elkin 1945: 59.
16. Ibid.: 74-75.
17. E.g., see Wittkover 1970: 156-157.
18. After Diószegi 1962: 162-163.
19. Neher 1962: 153. See also Neher 1961.
20. Neher 1962: 152-153.
21. Jilek 1974: 74-75.
22. Shirokogoroff 1935: 326, 329.
23. Ibid.: 326-327.
24. Ibid.
25. Nequatewa 1967: 133-134.
26. Cloutier 1973: 32-33, freely adapted from Bogoras 1909: 281.

Chapter 4: Power Animals

1. E.g., Gould 1969: 106; Stanner 1965; Warner 1958: 511.
2. Jelik 1974: 71; Cline 1938: 144.
3. Jelik 1974: 71.

4. Park 1938: 83.
5. See Harner 1972: 138-139.
6. Elkin 1945: 114.
7. See Castaneda 1972: 296-297; 299-300.
8. Lame Deer and Erdoes 1972: 136-137.
9. Spencer and Gillin 1927: 400.
10. Elkin 1945: 97.
11. Eliade 1964: 93.
12. Loeb 1926: 337.
13. Kroeber 1925: 200.
14. Harner 1973b: 140-145.
15. See Porta 1658.
16. Quoted in Harner 1973b: 142.
17. Castaneda 1968: 121-129; 1971: 122.
18. Eliade 1964: 128-129, especially following Andres 1938.
19. Jilek 1974: 25-26.
20. Ibid.: 92.
21. Boas 1916: 563.
22. Cloutier 1973: 57, freely adapted from Swanton 1909: 392.
23. Stewart 1946: 331-332.
24. Bunzel 1932: 531-532.
25. La Flesche 1925: 209. In the original song series, each stanza was repeated once.
26. Stewart 1946: 331, quoting R. Beals.
27. Wike 1941: 13.
28. E.g., Eliade 1964: 97-98.
29. Lame Deer and Erdoes 1972: 127.
30. Castaneda 1971: 185.
31. Eliade 1964: 99.
32. Foster 1944: 88-89.
33. See Castaneda 1974: 217. See also Foster 1944: 89.
34. Castaneda 1974: 118-270.
35. E.g., Castaneda 1974: 122-125, 132, 141. See Soustelle 1964: 196.
36. Foster 1944: 85-86, 95.
37. Teit 1900: 354; Eells 1889: 672-673.
38. See Harner 1972: 136.
39. See Benedict 1923.
40. Cline 1938: 141.
41. Ibid.
42. Ibid.: 142.

Chapter 5: The Journey to Restore Power

1. Haeberlin 1918: 249; Dorsey 1902: 234-236.
2. Haeberlin 1918: 250.
3. Jilek 1974: 71.
4. See Dorsey 1902; Frachtenberg 1920; Haeberlin 1918; and Waterman 1930.
5. Haeberlin 1918; Waterman 1930.
6. Waterman 1930: 137, 543.
7. Haeberlin 1918.
8. Ibid.
9. Eliade 1964: 226, 355-360.
10. Cawte 1974: 64; Reichel-Dolmatoff 1971: 172-174.
11. Wagley 1977: 181, 185-186.
12. Eliade 1964: 238.
13. Elkin 1945: 71.
14. E.g., Elkin 1945: 96, 143n; Cline 1938: 133.

15. Rasmussen 1929: 114.
16. Cloutier 1973: 67-68, freely adapted from Barbeau 1958: 53.
17. Oswalt 1964: 219, 221.
18. Eliade 1964: 254.
19. Cloutier 1973: 58-59, freely adapted from Barbeau 1951: 122.
20. Popov 1968: 138-139.

Chapter 6: Power Practice

1. Cline 1938: 136.
2. E.g., Park 1934: 104.
3. Cf. Harner 1972: 140; and Cline 1938: 145.
4. Lehtisalo 1924: 161.
5. Kensinger 1973: 12n.
6. Cline 1938: 145.
7. Warner 1958: 511; Wilbert 1972: 63.
8. Warner 1958: 511.
9. Probably the most elaborate practice of this technique was among the Iroquois. See Wallace 1958.
10. See Elkin 1945: 52-53.
11. Jelik 1974: 64-65.
12. Park 1934: 103.
13. E.g., see Culin 1907; Lesser 1978.
14. Elkin 1945: 44, 103, 120.
15. Elkin 1945: 44; Levi 1978: 43, 46.
16. Levi 1978: 42.
17. Elkin 1945: 42, 48.
18. Levi 1978: 49.
19. Elkin 1945: 97.
20. Ibid.: 29, 30, 32, 33, 47-48, 92, 94, 103, 122-125, 140.
21. Ibid.: 94.
22. Wilbert 1972: 65.
23. Wilbert 1973/1974: 93.
24. Furst 1973/74: 55; Prem Das, personal communication, 1980.
25. Ibid.
26. Elkin 1945: 44.
27. Ibid.: 107-108.
28. E.g., Levi 1978: 50.
29. Elkin 1945: 103.
30. Barbeau 1958: 73.
31. Elkin 1945: 108.
32. Ibid.: 110.
33. Barbeau 1958: 71.
34. Levi 1978: 50.
35. Ibid.: 47.
36. Castaneda 1978: 245.
37. The large quartz crystal shown in Kelly 1978: Fig. 5 was the one used. I am indebted to David Peri for providing information on Coast Miwok quartz crystal practice and belief.
38. Castaneda 1972: 291-302.
39. David Finkelstein, personal communication, 1980. I wish to acknowledge the assistance of Joan Halifax in obtaining this information.

Chapter 7: Extracting Harmful Intrusions

1. Popov 1968: 144.
2. Eliade 1964: 229.

3. The film is available from University Extension Films, University of California, Berkeley, CA 94720.
4. Mikhailowskii 1894: 141.
5. Lame Deer and Erdoes 1972: 134.
6. Cloutier 1973: 64-65, freely adapted from Barbeau 1958: 51-52.
7. Peri and Wharton, n.d.: 30, 34.
8. Oswalt 1964: 223, 225, 227, 229, 231. Mrs. Parrish noted that "some other doctors spit the disease out with the germs still alive" (Ibid.: 231n).
9. Amoss 1978: 14.
10. Katz 1976b: 82.
11. Ibid.: 86.

Afterword

1. Cousins 1979: 68-69.
2. Barbeau 1958: 48.
3. Carl Simonton, personal communication, 1980.
4. Simonton *et al.* 1978: 194-197.
5. Carl Simonton, personal communication, 1980.
6. Simonton *et al.* 1978: 7, 204.
7. Jochelson 1905: 47-54.
8. Printed with the author's kind permission.
9. Popov 1968: 143.

Appendix B

1. Merriam 1955: 315-319.
2. Boley 1973.

Preface References

Achterberg, Jeanne
    1985   *Imagery and Healing: Shamanism and Modern Medicine*. Boston: Shambhala Books.

Doore, Gary (compiler and ed.)
    1988   *Shaman's Path: Healing, Personal Growth, and Empowerment*. Boston: Shambhala Books.

Dossey, Larry
    1988   "The Inner Life of the Healer: The Importance of Shamanism for Modern Medicine." In *Shaman's Path: Healing, Personal Growth, and Empowerment* (Gary Doore, compiler and ed.), pp. 89–99. Boston: Shambhala Books.

Drury, Neville
    1989   *Elements of Shamanism*. Longmead, Shaftesbury, Dorset (United Kingdom): Element Books.

Eliade, Mircea
    1964   *Shamanism: Archaic Techniques of Ecstasy*. Bollingen Series 76. New York: Pantheon. Revised and enlarged from original French edition, 1951.

Foundation for Shamanic Studies Newsletter
    1988–   (Quarterly). Norwalk, Connecticut.

Grof, Stanislav
    1988   "The Shamanic Journey: Observations from Holotropic Therapy." In *Shaman's Path: Healing, Personal Growth, and Empowerment* (Gary Doore, compiler and ed.), pp. 161–175. Boston: Shambhala Books.

Harner, Michael
    1980   *The Way of the Shaman: A Guide to Power and Healing*. San Francisco: Harper and Row.

1982 *The Way of the Shaman: A Guide to Power and Healing.* Second edition. New York: Bantam Books.

1988 "Shamanic Counseling." In *Shaman's Path: Healing, Personal Growth, and Empowerment* (Gary Doore, compiler and ed.), pp. 179–187. Boston: Shambhala Books.

Lawlis, Frank

1988 "Shamanic Approaches in a Hospital Pain Clinic." In *Shaman's Path: Healing, Personal Growth, and Empowerment* (Gary Doore, compiler and ed.), pp. 139–149. Boston: Shambhala Books.

Nicholson, Shirley (compiler)

1987 *Shamanism: An Expanded View of Reality.* Wheaton, Illinois: Theosophical Publishing House.

Shaman's Drum: A Journal of Experiential Shamanism

1985– (Quarterly). Berkeley, California.

Townsend, Joan B.

1987 "Neo-Shamanism and the Modern Mystical Movement." In *Shaman's Path: Healing, Personal Growth, and Empowerment* (Gary Doore, compiler and ed.), pp. 73–83. Boston: Shambhala Books.

Bibliography

Amoss, Pamela
　1978　*Coast Salish Spirit Dancing: The Survival of an Ancestral Religion.*
　　　Seattle: University of Washington Press.
Andres, Friedrich
　1938　"Die Himmelreise der caräibischen Medizinmänner." *Zeitschrift für*
　　　Ethnologie 70: 3-5, 331-342.
Ashaninga, Kecizate
　1977　"The Chain of Worlds." As told to Fernando Llosa Porras. *Parabola*
　　　2 (3): 58-62.
Ballard, Arthur C.
　1929　*Mythology of Southern Puget Sound.* University of Washington
　　　Publications in Anthropology 3 (2): 31-150.
Barbeau, Marius
　1951　"Tsimshyan Songs." In *The Tsimshian: Their Arts and Music* (Viola
　　　E. Garfield *et al.*), American Ethnological Society Publication 18.
　1958　*Medicine-Men on the North Pacific Coast.* National Museum of
　　　Canada Bulletin No. 152 (Anthropological Series No. 42). Ottawa:
　　　Department of Northern Affairs and National Resources.
Benedict, Ruth F.
　1923　*The Concept of the Guardian Spirit in North America.* Memoirs of
　　　the American Anthropological Association, 29. Menasha, Wisconsin.
Biesele, Marguerite Anne
　1975　*Folklore and Ritual of !Kung Hunter-Gatherers.* Ph.D. dissertation
　　　in anthropology, Harvard University. Cambridge, Massachusetts.
Boas, Franz
　1900　*The Mythology of the Bella Coola Indians.* Memoirs of the Ameri-
　　　can Museum of Natural History, Vol. 2: 25-127.

1916   *Tsimshian Mythology*. Bureau of American Ethnology, Thirty-first Annual Report, 1909-1910. Washington: Smithsonian Institution.

Bogoras, Waldemar
1909   *The Chukchee*. Memoirs of the American Museum of Natural History, Vol. 11 (Franz Boas, ed.). Reprints from Vol. 7 of the Jesup North Pacific Expedition, 1904-1909. Leiden: E. J. Brill.

Boley, Raymond
1973   [Recording] *Stick Game Songs: A Live Recording of a Stick Game in Progress during the Arlee Pow Wow, Flathead Indian Reservation, Montana, July, 1972*. Phoenix, Arizona: Canyon Records.

Bunzel, Ruth L.
1932   "Introduction to Zuñi Ceremonialism." *Bureau of American Ethnology, Forty-seventh Annual Report, 1929-1930*, pp. 467-544. Washington: Smithsonian Institution.

Castaneda, Carlos
1968   *The Teachings of Don Juan: A Yaqui Way of Knowledge*. Berkeley and Los Angeles: University of California Press.
1971   *A Separate Reality: Further Conversations with Don Juan*. New York: Simon and Schuster.
1972   *Journey to Ixtlan: The Lessons of Don Juan*. New York: Simon and Schuster.
1974   *Tales of Power*. New York: Simon and Schuster.

Cawte, John
1974   *Medicine is the Law: Studies in Psychiatric Anthropology of Australian Tribal Societies*. Honolulu: University Press of Hawaii.

Cline, Walter
1938   "Religion and World View." In *The Sinkaietk or Southern Okanagon of Washington* (Leslie Spier, ed.), pp. 133-182. General Series in Anthropology, No. 6 (Contributions from the Laboratory of Anthropology, 2). Menasha, Wisconsin: Banta.

Cloutier, David
1973   *Spirit, Spirit: Shaman Songs, Incantations*. Versions based on texts recorded by anthropologists. Providence, Rhode Island: Copper Beech Press.

Cousins, Norman
1979   *Anatomy of an Illness as Perceived by the Patient: Reflections on Healing and Regeneration*. New York: Norton.

Culin, Stewart
1907   *Games of the North American Indians*. Bureau of American Ethnology Annual Report 24: 29-809. Washington: Smithsonian Institution.

Devereux, George
1957   "Dream Learning and Individual Ritual Differences in Mohave Shamanism." *American Anthropologist* 59: 1036-1045.

Diószegi, Vilmos
1962   "Tuva Shamanism: Intraethnic Differences and Interethnic Analogies." *Acta Etnographica* 11:143-190.

159

Dorsey, George A.
  1902   "The Dwamish Indian Spirit Boat and Its Use." *Free Museum of Science and Art Bulletin* 3 (4): 227-238. Philadelphia.

Eells, Myron
  1889   "The Twana, Chemakum, and Klallam Indians, of Washington Territory." *Annual Report of the Smithsonian Institution for Year Ending 1887,* Part I, pp. 605-681. Washington.

Eliade, Mircea
  1964   *Shamanism: Archaic Techniques of Ecstasy.* Bollingen Series 76. New York: Pantheon. Revised and enlarged from original French edition, 1951.

Elkin, A. P.
  1945   *Aboriginal Men of High Degree.* The John Murtagh Macrossan Memorial Lectures for 1944, University of Queensland. Sydney: Australasian Publishing.

  1977   *Aboriginal Men of High Degree.* Second edition. New York: St. Martin's Press.

Foster, George M.
  1944   "Nagualism in Mexico and Guatemala." *Acta Americana* 2: 85-103.

Frachtenberg, Leo J.
  1920   "Eschatology of the Quileute Indians." *American Anthropologist* 22: 330-340.

Furst, Peter T.
  1973/   "The Roots and Continuities of Shamanism." *Artscanada,* Nos. 184-
  1974   187. Thirtieth Anniversary Issue, Stones, Bones and Skin: Ritual and Shamanic Art: 33-60.

Furst, Peter T. (ed.)
  1972   *Flesh of the Gods: The Ritual Use of Hallucinogens.* New York: Praeger.

Gayton, A. H.
  1935   "The Orpheus Myth in North America." *Journal of American Folklore* 48: 263-293.

Gould, Richard A.
  1969   *Yiwara: Foragers of the Australian Desert.* New York: Scribner's.

Haeberlin, Herman K.
  1918   "SBeTeTDA'Q, a Shamanistic Performance of the Coast Salish." *American Anthropologist* 20 (3): 249-257.

Halifax, Joan (ed.)
  1979   *Shamanic Voices: A Survey of Visionary Narratives.* New York: Dutton.

Harner, Michael J.
  1968   "The Sound of Rushing Water." *Natural History* 77 (6): 28-33; 60-61.

  1972   *The Jívaro: People of the Sacred Waterfalls.* Garden City: Doubleday/Natural History Press.

  1973a   "The Sound of Rushing Water." In *Hallucinogens and Shamanism* (Michael J. Harner, ed.), pp. 15-27. New York: Oxford University Press. Originally published 1968.

1973b   "The Role of Hallucinogenic Plants in European Witchcraft." In *Hallucinogens and Shamanism* (Michael J. Harner, ed.), pp. 125-150. New York: Oxford University Press.

Harner, Michael J. (ed.)
1973c   *Hallucinogens and Shamanism.* New York: Oxford University Press.

Howitt, A. W.
1904   *The Native Tribes of South-East Australia.* London: Macmillan.

Hultkrantz, Åke
1973   "A Definition of Shamanism." *Temenos* 9:25-37.
1979   *The Religions of the American Indian.* Translated by Monica Setterwall from the 1967 Swedish edition and revised. Berkeley and Los Angeles: University of California Press.

Jilek, Wolfgang G.
1974   *Salish Indian Mental Health and Culture Change: Psychohygienic and Therapeutic Aspects of the Guardian Spirit Ceremonial.* Toronto and Montreal: Holt, Rinehart and Winston of Canada.

Jochelson, Waldemar
1905   *Religion and Myths of the Koryak.* Memoirs of the American Museum of Natural History, Vol. 10. Leiden: E. J. Brill; New York: G. E. Stechert.

Katz, Richard
1976a   "Education for Transcendence: !Kia-Healing with the Kalahari !Kung." In *Kalahari Hunter-Gatherers: Studies of the !Kung San and their Neighbors* (Richard B. Lee and Irven DeVore, eds.), pp. 281-301. Cambridge: Harvard University Press.
1976b   "The Painful Ecstasy of Healing." *Psychology Today* (December): 81-86.

Kelly, Isabel
1978   "Coast Miwok." In *Handbook of North American Indians,* Vol. 8, *California* (Robert F. Heizer, vol. ed.; William C. Sturtevant, gen. ed.), pp. 414-425. Washington: Smithsonian Institution.

Kensinger, Kenneth M.
1973   *"Banisteriopsis* Usage Among the Peruvian Cashinahua." In *Hallucinogens and Shamanism* (Michael J. Harner, ed.), pp. 9-14. New York: Oxford University Press.

Kroeber, A. L.
1925   *Handbook of the Indians of California.* Bureau of American Ethnology Bulletin 78. Washington: Smithsonian Institution.

La Flesche, Francis
1925   "The Osage Tribe: The Rite of Vigil." *Bureau of American Ethnology, Thirty-ninth Annual Report, 1917-1918,* pp. 31-630. Washington: Smithsonian Institution.

Lame Deer, John (Fire), and Richard Erdoes
1972   *Lame Deer: Seeker of Visions.* New York: Simon and Schuster.

Lehtisalo, Toivo V.
1924   *Entwurf einer Mythologie der Jurak-Samojeden.* Mémoires de la Société Finno-Ougrienne, 53. Helsinki.

Lesser, Alexander
1978   *The Pawnee Ghost Dance Hand Game: Ghost Dance Revival and Ethnic Identity*. Madison: University of Wisconsin Press. Originally published 1933.
Levi, Jerome Meyer
1978   *"Wii'ipay:* The Living Rocks—Ethnographic Notes on Crystal Magic Among some California Yumans." *Journal of California Anthropology* 5 (1): 42-52.
Lewis, I. M.
1971   *Ecstatic Religion*. Harmondsworth: Penguin.
Loeb, Edwin M.
1926   *Pomo Folkways*. University of California Publications in American Archaeology and Ethnology, Vol. 19, pp. 149-405. Berkeley.
Lowie, Robert H.
1952   *Primitive Religion*. New York: Grosset and Dunlap. Originally published 1924.
Ludwig, Arnold M.
1972   "Altered States of Consciousness." In *Altered States of Consciousness* (Charles T. Tart, ed.), second edition, pp. 11-24. New York: Anchor/Doubleday.
Mandell, Arnold J.
1978   "The Neurochemistry of Religious Insight and Ecstasy." In *Art of the Huichol Indians* (Kathleen Berrin, ed.), pp. 71-81. New York: Fine Arts Museums of San Francisco/Harry N. Abrams.
Mc.Gregor, John C.
1941   *Southwestern Archaeology*. New York: John Wiley.
Merriam, Alan P.
1955   "The Hand Game of the Flathead Indians." *Journal of American Folklore* 68: 313-324.
Mikhailowskii, V. M.
1894   "Shamanism in Siberia and European Russia." *Journal of the Royal Anthropological Institute of Great Britain and Ireland* 24: 62-100, 126-158. Translated from the Russian original, published 1892.
Neher, Andrew
1961   "Auditory Driving Observed with Scalp Electrodes in Normal Subjects." *Electroencephalography and Clinical Neurophysiology* 13 (3): 449-451.
1962   "A Physiological Explanation of Unusual Behavior in Ceremonies Involving Drums." *Human Biology* 34 (2): 151-160.
Nequatewa, Edmund
1967   *Truth of a Hopi*. Flagstaff, Arizona: Northland. Originally published as Museum of Northern Arizona Bulletin 8 in 1936.
Oswalt, Robert L.
1964   *Kashaya Texts*. University of California Publications in Linguistics, Vol. 36. Berkeley and Los Angeles.
Park, Willard Z.
1934   "Paviotso Shamanism." *American Anthropologist* 36: 98-113.

1938   *Shamanism in Western North America: A Study of Cultural Rela-
        tionships.* Northwestern University Studies in the Social Sciences,
        No. 2. Evanston and Chicago: Northwestern University.

Peri, David, and Robert Wharton
n.d.   *Sucking Doctor—Second Night: Comments by Doctor, Patient, and
        Singers.* Unpublished manuscript.

Popov, A. A.
1968   "How Sereptie Djaruoskin of the Nganasans (Tavgi Samoyeds) Be-
        came a Shaman." In *Popular Beliefs and Folklore Tradition in Sibe-
        ria* (V. Diószegi, ed.), pp. 137-145. English translation revised by
        Stephen P. Dunn. Indiana University Publications, Uralic and Altaic
        Series, Vol. 57, Thomas A. Sebeok, ed. Bloomington: Indiana Univer-
        sity, and The Hague: Mouton.

Porta, Giovanni Battista (John Baptista Porta)
1658   *Natural Magick.* Translated from the expurgated Italian edition of
        1589, which was based on the German edition of 1562. Reproduction
        of the 1658 English edition. New York: Basic Books. 1957.

Rasmussen, Knud
1929   *Intellectual Culture of the Iglulik Eskimos.* Report of the Fifth
        Thule Expedition 1921-24, Vol. 7, No. 1. Copenhagen: Gyldendalske
        Boghandel, Nordisk Forlag.

Ray, Verne F.
1963   *Primitive Pragmatists: The Modoc Indians of Northern California.*
        Seattle: University of Washington Press.

Reichel-Dolmatoff, Gerardo
1971   *Amazonian Cosmos: The Sexual and Religious Symbolism of the
        Tukano Indians.* Translated by the author from the original 1968
        Spanish language edition. Chicago: University of Chicago Press.

Reinhard, Johan
1975   "Shamanism and Spirit Possession." In *Spirit Possession in the Ne-
        pal Himalayas* (John Hitchcock and Rex Jones, eds.), pp. 12-18.
        Warminster: Aris and Phillips.

Shirokogoroff, S. M.
1935   *Psychomental Complex of the Tungus.* London: Kegan Paul, Trench,
        Trubner.

Simonton, O. Carl, Stephanie Matthews-Simonton, and James Creighton
1978   *Getting Well Again: A Step-by-Step Self-Help Guide to Overcoming
        Cancer for Patients and Their Families.* Los Angeles: J. P. Tarcher;
        New York: St. Martin's Press.

Soustelle, Jacques
1964   *Daily Life of the Aztecs on the Eve of the Spanish Conquest.* Trans-
        lated from the French by Patrick O'Brian. Harmondsworth: Penguin.

Spencer, Walter Baldwin, and F. J. Gillen
1927   *The Arunta: A Study of a Stone Age People.* 2 vols. London: Mac-
        millan.

Spott, Robert, and A. L. Kroeber
1942   *Yurok Narratives.* University of California Publications in American
        Archaeology and Ethnology 35: 143-256. Berkeley and Los Angeles.

Stanner, W. E. H.
1965   "The Dreaming." In *Reader in Comparative Religion: An Anthropological Approach* (William A. Lessa and Evon Z. Vogt, eds.), second edition, pp. 158-167. New York: Harper and Row. Originally published 1956 in *Australian Signpost* (T. A. G. Hungerford, ed.), pp. 51-65. Melbourne: F. W. Cheshire.

Stewart, Kenneth M.
1946   "Spirit Possession in Native America." *Southwestern Journal of Anthropology* 2: 323-339.

Sverdrup, Harald U.
1938   *With the People of the Tundra*. Oslo: Gyldendal Norsk Forlag.

Swanton, John R.
1909   *Tlingit Myths and Texts*. Bureau of American Ethnology Bulletin 39. Washington: Smithsonian Institution.

Teit, James
1900   *The Thompson Indians of British Columbia*. Anthropology 1, the Jesup North Pacific Expedition. Memoirs of the American Museum of Natural History, Vol. 2, No. 4. New York.

Vastokas, Joan M.
1973/   "The Shamanic Tree of Life." *Artscanada,* Nos. 184-187. Thirtieth
1974   Anniversary Issue, Stones, Bones and Skin: Ritual and Shamanic Art: 125-149.

Wagley, Charles
1977   *Welcome of Tears: the Tapirapé Indians of Central Brazil*. New York: Oxford University Press.

Wallace, Anthony F. C.
1958   "Dreams and Wishes of the Soul: A Type of Psychoanalytic Theory Among the Seventeenth Century Iroquois." *American Anthropologist* 60 (2): 234-248.

Warner, W. Lloyd
1958   *A Black Civilization: A Social Study of an Australian Tribe*. Revised edition. New York: Harper.

Waterman, T. T.
1930   "The Paraphernalia of the Duwamish 'Spirit-Canoe' Ceremony." *Indian Notes, Museum of the American Indian* 7: 129-148; 295-312; 535-561.

Weiss, Gerald
1972   "Campa Cosmology." *Ethnology* 11 (2): 157-172.
1975   *Campa Cosmology*. Anthropological Papers of the American Museum of Natural History 52 (5): 219-588.

Wike, Joyce A.
1941   *Modern Spirit Dancing of Northern Puget Sound*. M.A. thesis in anthropology, University of Washington. Seattle.

Wilbert, Johannes
1972   "Tobacco and Shamanistic Ecstasy Among the Warao Indians of Venezuela." In *Flesh of the Gods: The Ritual Use of Hallucinogens* (Peter T. Furst, ed.), pp. 55-83. New York: Praeger.

1973/   "The Calabash of the Ruffled Feathers." *Artscanada,* Nos. 184-187.
1974   Thirtieth Anniversary Issue, Stones, Bones and Skin: Ritual and Shamanic Art: 90-93.

Wilson, Norman L., and Arlean H. Towne
1978   "Nisenan." In *Handbook of North American Indians* (William C. Sturtevant, gen. ed.), Vol. 8: *California* (Robert F. Heizer, ed.), pp. 387-397. Washington: Smithsonian Institution.

Wittkower, E. D.
1970   "Trance and Possesssion States." *International Journal of Social Psychiatry* 16 (2): 153-160.

Index

Mohave woman, 46
Montana, 108, 144
Murngin people, 98–99

Nagual animal, 42, 63
Natural Magick (Porta), 60
Natural selection, *xiv–xv*
Nature, 54
Navaho reservation, 102
Neher, Andrew, 51–52
Nevada Indians, 104
North American Indians, 18, 49, 54; and bone game, 103, 104, 108, 144; and dreams, 100; and drumming, 52; and entrance to Lowerworld, 25, 26–28; and guardian spirits, 42, 58–64 *passim,* 70–71, 72, 85–98 *passim,* 132, 134; and healing, 116, 118, 125–30, 136, 137, 138; and power songs, 74–75, 85–86; and quartz crystals, 109, 111, 112. *See also* Eskimo

Okanagon Indians, 58, 64
Ordinary State of Consciousness (OSC), *xiii–xv,* 21, 24, 47–48, 50, 53, 54, 123
Osage Indian song, 62
Oswalt, Robert L., 126

Paiute Indians, 104
Paipai shamans, 111
Parrish, Essie, 74–75, 116, 125–30
Paviotso Indians, 104
Peru, 97. *See also* Conibo Indians
Piripiri juice, 17
Plains Indians, 63, 64, 87, 95
Plants, 113–15, 116–17
Pomo Indians, 18, 26, 74
Porta, Giovanni Battista, 60
Power animals, 43, 57–72, 76–103, 123. *See also* Guardian spirits
Power intrusions, 17–18, 115–34, 137
Power objects, 17, 108–12, 116–17
Power songs, 53, 72–75; in bone game, 106; and power animal recovery, 70, 72, 77–78, 92, 102; and power intrusions, 117, 119–20, 121, 123, 127, 131, 132, 133, 134
Professional shamanism, 139
Pueblo Indians, 27–28, 54, 61–62

Quartz crystals, 23, 109–12

Rasmussen, Knud, 25–26, 73

Rattles, 50–51, 52–53, 142–43; and power animals, 65–67, 76, 77, 78, 81, 85, 91, 92, 102; and power intrusions, 119–21, 123, 131, 133; quartz crystals in, 110
Reinhard, Johan, 49–50
Rock-seeing, 54–55

Salish Indians, 18; and bone game, 104, 144; and drumming, 52; and healing, 132, 134; and power animals, 58, 60–61, 62, 70–71, 91, 95, 98
Samoyed shamans, 26, 93–94, 97, 115, 117, 139
Sangay, 9
Scandinavia, 49, 60
Schweitzer, Albert, 135
"Se Pa Po Nah," 28
Sevilla del Oro, 8
Sex (gender): and shamanic aptitude, 43
Shamanic enlightenment, 22–24, 139
Shamanic State of Consciousness (SSC), *xiii–xv, xvi,* 21–39, 46–56; and power animals, 58, 59, 66–67; and quartz crystals, 109. *See also* Journeys, shamanic
Shamanism (Eliade), 41
Shirokogoroff, S. M., 53
Siberian shamans, 20, 24, 49, 55–56, 71, 139; and death/rebirth experiences, *xii;* and drumming, 51, 52, 53, 78; and entrance to Lowerworld, 26; and foreseeing, 97; and guardian spirits, 42, 60, 78, 93–94; and plants, 115; and power songs, 117
Simonton, O. Carl, 137
Singing. *See* Power songs
Sinkaietk Indians, 95, 98. *See also* Okanagon Indians
Sioux Indians, 18, 54, 59, 118, 130
Sipapu holes, 27–28
Sleeping, 98–99
South American Indians, 41, 49; foreseeing by, 97; and guardian spirits, 43, 58–76 *passim,* 95, 96, 99, 101–2; and medical doctors, 137; and quartz crystals, 109, 110, 111; and sleeping, 98. *See also* Conibo Indians; Jívaro Indians
South Dakota, 18, 130
Soyot (Tuvas) people, 51
Spirit canoe, 70–71, 89, 91–94, 119
Spirit helpers, 16–18, 43, 93, 113–15, 116–23, 130

169

About the Author

Michael Harner, Ph.D., has practiced shamanism and shamanic healing since 1961, and pioneered their return to contemporary life, publicly teaching shamanic methods since the early 1970s. Founder and director of the Foundation for Shamanic Studies in Norwalk, Connecticut, he is former professor and chairperson of the Department of Anthropology at the Graduate Faculty of the New School for Social Research in New York, and has taught at the University of California, Berkeley, where he received his Ph.D., and at Columbia and Yale, as well as having served as co-chairperson of the Anthropology Section of the New York Academy of Sciences. He has done fieldwork in the Upper Amazon, Mexico, western North America, the Canadian Arctic, and Samiland (Lapland). His books include *The Jívaro, Hallucinogens and Shamanism,* and a novel, *Cannibal,* which he co-authored. He teaches shamanic training workshops and courses worldwide.